The
Final
Countdown

THIRD PRINTING

Billy Crone

Cover Design:
KEVIN BISH

To my wife, Brandie.

Thank you for being so patient
with a man full of dreams.
You truly are my gift from God.
It is an honor to have you as my wife
and I'm still amazed that you willingly chose
to join me in this challenging yet exhilarating
roller coaster ride called the Christian life.
God has truly done exceedingly abundantly above all
that we could have ever asked or even thought of.
Who ever said that living for the Lord was boring, huh?
One day our ride together will be over here on earth.
Yet it will continue on in eternity forever.
I love you.

Contents

Preface

Unfortunately, in the Church today, the study of prophecy has been forsaken under the assumption that one can't really know for sure what it all means and therefore we should refrain from teaching it. Yet, when you think about it, this is actually a slap in the face to God; for a majority of the Holy Scriptures deal directly or indirectly with prophetic issues. Why would God put prophecy in the Bible if it wasn't meant to be understood? Do we dare say that He is playing cat and mouse with us? In addition, how can one say that they are being faithful to present the whole counsel of God when they leave a major portion of it, prophecy, out of the picture?

Furthermore, Bible prophecy has a wonderful way of bringing home two crucial truths that seem to be long forgotten in the American Church. One truth is that this world is not going to last forever. A flood destroyed it the first time and the next time it will be by fire. Therefore, this forces you and I the Christian to stop living merely for the temporary things of this world, thus wasting our lives, and instead to get busy storing up treasures in heaven, which last forever. And boy, is that not needed today!

Also, Bible prophecy drives home the second truth of God being absolutely sovereign. He is in full control of all things at all times. So much so that God has already mapped out mankind's history. Therefore, only the student of Bible prophecy can rightly discern the times in which we live. And best of all, because God is sovereign, no matter how uncomfortable things may get, we can still be at peace knowing that our Lord reigns and that He will soon return to take us to be with Him.

What you are about to read will most assuredly shock you and certainly push you out of your comfort zone. If it doesn't, then you might want to check your pulse. And, lest you think I'm making this stuff up, I invite you to check it out for yourself. This is why everything has been meticulously documented. Folks, this is not a time to react in fear but in faith. Our hope is not to be here, but in heaven. And remember, God is sovereign! One last piece of advice; when you are through reading this book then will you please **READ YOUR BIBLE**? I mean that in the nicest possible way. Enjoy, and I'm looking forward to seeing you someday!

Billy Crone
2008

Chapter One

The Jewish People

Now, I don't know about you guys, but **I've noticed** how most people in our society today have basically become self-centered. And because of this, everybody walks around with the "poor me" syndrome. They act as if **their problems** are the biggest and worst of all, when in reality they're just being blown out of proportion to draw attention. Therefore, in light of this trend in our society, how does one know if they're **really** having a bad day versus just exaggerating about themselves? Great question! I'm glad you asked. You see, I came across a list of some genuine signs to indicate that you are really having a **truly bad day**. In fact, if any of these have happened to you, there would be no need to ask the question. You're having a bad day.

1. Your secretary tells you the FBI is on line 1, the DA is on line 2, and CBS is on line 3.
2. Your suggestion box starts ticking.
3. The plumber floats by on your kitchen table.
4. The simple instructions enclosed, aren't.
5. You wake to discover your waterbed has sprung a leak and then realize you don't have a waterbed.
6. You wake up face down on the pavement.

7. Your birthday cake collapses from the weight of the candles.
8. People send your wife sympathy cards on your anniversary.
9. Your wife says "Good Morning, Bill" and your name is George.
10. You're driving on the freeway when you car horn not only accidentally goes off but it remains stuck behind a group of Hells Angels.[1]

Yes, having your horn get stuck behind a group of Hells Angels would definitely be a bad day, wouldn't it? But, believe it or not, there's a worse day than that. You see, the **ultimate sign** that you're headed for the worst day of your life would have to be this; it's when you wake up one morning only to realize that your family has disappeared. You run to turn on your TV to see what's happening and there you watch a special worldwide news report declaring that millions of people all over the globe are missing. Then, as you spy the Bible on the coffee table, it suddenly dawns on you that your family was right after all when they kept telling you about the rapture of the Church. Then to your horror, you realize that **you've been left behind** and have been catapulted into the seven-year Tribulation that is coming upon the whole world.

And folks, the time of the Tribulation is not a party. It's an outpouring of God's wrath on a wicked and rebellious planet. In fact Jesus said in **Matthew 24** that it would be a time of greater horror than anything the world has ever seen or will ever see again. He also said that unless that time of calamity is shortened, the entire human race would be destroyed. But God is not only a God of wrath; He's a God of love as well. And **because He loves you and I**, He has given us many warning signs that the Tribulation could be near and Christ's 2nd Coming is rapidly approaching. Therefore, to keep you and I from experiencing the ultimate bad day of being left behind, we're going to take a look at what the Bible declares to you and I as **The Final Countdown**.

We're going to observe **10 signs** given by God to lovingly wake us up so we can give our lives to Him before it's too late. So let's get started. The **#10** sign on **The Final Countdown** is none other than **The Jewish People**. One of the first and most important prophetic events on God's end-time calendar is concerning the Jewish people. In **minute detail**, the Lord prophesied specific events that would happen to Israel, giving a clear indication that we could be in the last days. So just what are these specific prophesies being fulfilled today concerning **The Jewish People**? Well, I'm glad you asked. The **1st End Time Prophecy** concerning **The Jewish People** is that **Israel would return to the land**.

Isaiah 43:5-6 "Do not be afraid, for I am with you. I will gather you and your children from east and west and from north and south. I will bring my sons and daughters back to Israel from the distant corners of the earth." (NLT)

Ever since the destruction of the Jewish Temple in 70 AD, the Jewish people have been scattered all over the earth. But **in the last century alone**, millions of Jews have returned to Israel, fulfilling this prophecy. In fact, just like the Bible said, they came specifically from the east, the west, the north, and the south. First from the **East**, in the **early 1900's** many Jews living in the Middle East moved to Israel. Then from the **West**, during **mid-1900's**, hundreds of thousands of Jews living in the West (Europe and the United States) began moving to Israel. Then from the **North, during the 1980's**, Russia finally began to allow hundreds of thousands of Jews to return to Israel. And next from the **South**, Israel struck a deal with Ethiopia's communist government. And on the weekend of **May 25, 1991**, 14,500 Ethiopian Jews were airlifted to Israel. And more and more Jews are returning to Israel each year from all over the world. First from the East, West, North, and then South.[2] Just like the Bible said! When? In the last days.

The **2nd End Time Prophecy** concerning **The Jewish People** is that **Israel would become a nation again**.

Isaiah 11:11-12 "In that day the Lord will bring back a remnant of his people for the second time, returning them to the land of Israel from Assyria, Lower Egypt, Upper Egypt, Ethiopia, Elam, Babylonia, Hamath, and all the distant coastlands. He will raise a flag among the nations for Israel to rally around. He will gather the scattered people of Judah from the ends of the earth." (NLT)

Since 721 BC approximately 14 different peoples have possessed the land of Israel. Yet, as the Bible said, the nation of Israel would be reborn. One day they would regain their independence. And can anyone guess what happened on **May 14, 1948**? That's right! After waiting centuries, the people who were scattered all over the world, not only returned to their land, but they also **became a nation**. From out of nowhere and against all odds, Israel was reborn. And in 1967 the Jewish people even recaptured the city of Jerusalem. Just like the Bible said! When? In the last days.

The **3rd End Time Prophecy** concerning **The Jewish People** is that **Israel would be brought forth in one day**.

Isaiah 66:8 "Who has ever seen or heard of anything as strange as this? Has a nation ever been born in a single day? Has a country ever come forth in a mere moment? But by the time Jerusalem's birth pains begin, the baby will be born; the nation will come forth." (NLT)

On the morning of May 14, 1948, at precisely 4pm, the members of the People's Council signed the proclamation and the declaration was made that, "The State of Israel is established. This meeting is ended." Israel not only became a nation, but also was literally brought forth as a nation **in one day**.[3] Just like the Bible said! When? In the last days.

The **4th End Time Prophecy** concerning **The Jewish People** is that **Israel would be a united nation again**.

Ezekiel 37:21-22 "And give them this message from the Sovereign LORD: I will gather the people of Israel from among the nations. I will bring them home to their own land from the places where they have been scattered. I will unify them into one nation in the land. One king will rule them all; no longer will they be divided into two nations." (NLT)

In about 926 BC, the Jewish people became a divided nation. The Northern ten tribes were called Israel, and the Southern two tribes were called Judah. But when the Jews regained independence in 1948, for the first time in 2900 years, Israel was again united as a **single nation**, not two.[4] Just like the Bible said! When? In the last days.

The **5th End Time Prophecy** concerning **The Jewish People** is that **Israel's currency would be the shekel**.

Ezekiel 45:12,13,16 "The standard unit for weight will be the silver shekel. This is the tax you must give to the prince. All the people of Israel must join the prince in bringing their offerings." (NLT)

The Bible predicted that in their future temple sacrifices, the people of Israel would be paying their taxes in shekels. But the problem is that Israel's currency wasn't the shekel, it was the pound. However, that all changed in **1980**. This was when the shekel was brought back into existence as Israel's official currency and is still being used right up to this day.[5] Just like the Bible said! When? In the last days.

The **6th End Time Prophecy** concerning **The Jewish People** is that **Israel would blossom as a rose in the desert**.

Isaiah 35:1-2 "Even the wilderness will rejoice in those days. The desert will blossom with flowers. Yes, there will be an abundance of flowers and singing and joy! The deserts will become as green as the mountains of Lebanon, as lovely as Mount Carmel's pastures and the plain of Sharon. There the LORD will display his glory, the splendor of our God." (NLT)

When Mark Twain visited Israel in the 1860's, he reported that Israel was a barren wasteland with no trees. Almost 2000 years of foreign conquerors had abused the land, leaving it as a desert wasteland. But when the Jews began to return, they built a network of irrigation systems. Today, there are over **400 million trees** in Israel and as a result, rainfall has increased over 450 percent. In fact, Israel, the former desert, is now the breadbasket of the Middle East and is exporting fruit all over the world. Then, Israel diverted the water from the Sea of Galilee and channeled it through sections of the deserts, which have allowed the deserts to literally begin to **blossom** with an abundance of flowers, which are now, along with ornamental plants, also being exported all over the world.[6] Just like the Bible said! When? In the last days.

The **7th End Time Prophecy** concerning **The Jewish People** is that **Israel would have a powerful military**.

Zechariah 12:6 "On that day I will make the leaders of Judah like a firepot in a woodpile, like a flaming torch among sheaves. They will consume right and left all the surrounding peoples, but Jerusalem will remain intact in her place." (NLT)

Outnumbered and against all odds, Israeli forces have astounded the world by their victories during six wars. For instance, within hours of Israel's declaration of independence in 1948, Egypt, Syria, Jordan, Iraq, and Lebanon all invaded Israel. The combined population of those countries was at least **twenty million** at that time. Yet, Israel had fewer than **one million** in population. But when all was said and done, the Jewish people not only won the war, but they expanded the size of Israel by fifty percent. Today, Israel is indeed one of the most powerful military forces in the world, with full nuclear capabilities. Hands down, they are the most powerful force in the region.[7] Just like the Bible said! When? In the last days.

The **8ᵗʰ End Time Prophecy** concerning **The Jewish People** is that **Israel would be a center of conflict to the whole world**.

Zechariah 12:2-3 "I am going to make Jerusalem a cup that sends all the surrounding peoples reeling. Judah will be besieged as well as Jerusalem. On that day, when all the nations of the earth are gathered against her, I will make Jerusalem an immovable rock for all the nations. All who try to move it will injure themselves." (NIV)

In 1948, when the Jewish people became a nation, **the very next day,** the nations around them declared war with Israel. And the fighting for control has never stopped. Also, Israel's location in the heart of the world's oil reserves makes it a great **strategic significance** to all the countries in the world. Then, to make matters worse, the world's three largest religions have headquarters where? **In Jerusalem**! This is why you can daily turn on the news and read in all the newspapers of how Israel has indeed become an **international problem**. Just like the Bible said! When? In the last days.

The **9ᵗʰ End Time Prophecy** concerning **The Jewish People** is that **Israel would rebuild the temple**.

Revelation 11:2 "Leave out the court which is outside the temple and do not measure it, for it has been given to the nations; and they will tread under foot the holy city for forty-two months." (NAS)

The book of Revelation clearly reveals that a Jewish temple will be in existence during the time of the Tribulation. And can you guess who is preparing to build another temple **right now**? But the problem is that the Muslim Dome of the Rock is sitting right where many believe the previous temple was and where the new proposed temple needs to be. This is one of the reasons why there is such strife in Jerusalem today. But strife or not, the Bible is clear, in the end-time, the temple **will be rebuilt**. In fact, many scholars believe that it will occur as a result of a peace treaty made with the antichrist himself.

Daniel 9:27 "He will make a treaty with the people for a period of one set of seven, but after half this time, he will put an end to the sacrifices and offerings." (NLT)

It is in this passage that we not only see that the Tribulation will last seven years, but its also where some feel that the antichrist with his false miracles and fabulous charisma will be the **only one** to convince Israel to give up more land and the **carrot he uses** is the permission to rebuild the Temple. But even if they don't get permission to build it where the current Dome of the Rock is, it just so happens that **right now** Jewish archaeologists are saying the actual site for the temple may very well not be where the Dome of the Rock is, but rather to the North or the South of it, which means they could build it right now even with the current location of the Dome of the Rock![8]

However, it's important to know that the Jewish people aren't looking 100 years down the road to rebuild the Temple. People, the blueprints for the temple are ready today. In fact, a group in Israel called the **Temple Institute** is **right now** training priests to serve in the new Temple. They have even reconstructed most of the clothing and vessels that are required for worship in the new Temple. In fact, things are getting so close that for the first time since the articles of the Temple we're hauled away at the destruction of Jerusalem in 70 A.D., the Golden Menorah has not only been reconstructed at the cost of two million dollars, but it has been relocated opposite the Temple Mount. Furthermore, even more recent, the golden crown of the Jewish High priest has finally been completed, where it is waiting to be placed on the "right head" at the "right time" to begin the Temple services.[9] Therefore, almost everything is ready for the new Temple with the exception of one item, a red heifer. You see, the ashes of a pure red heifer are needed for cleansing.

Numbers 19:1-4 "The LORD said to Moses and Aaron: This is a requirement of the law that the LORD has commanded: Tell the Israelites to bring you a red heifer without defect or blemish and that has never been under a yoke. Give it to Eleazar the priest; it is to be taken outside the camp and slaughtered in his presence. Then Eleazar the priest is to take some of its blood on his finger and sprinkle it seven times toward the front of the Tent of Meeting." (NIV)

You see, according to Bible, the ashes of a pure red heifer are needed to perform the necessary purification or cleaning rituals that are a part of the service of the Temple. But the problem is, since the Temple was destroyed by the Romans in 70 AD, pure red heifers no longer exist, **until now**. Believe it or not, a red heifer was born in Israel just a few years ago.[10] And even though it ended up having a slight blemish, and was hence disqualified, it just so happens they're starting to appear on the scene after all these years! Then, even if it doesn't happen **naturally**, we just happen to be living in the days when for the first time in man's history, we could create a red heifer **artificially** through genetic engineering and cloning!

Then, to make matters even more interesting, for the first time in 1,600 we have the rebirth of the Jewish Sanhedrin, just a couple years ago.[11] And the Jewish people right now are expecting the return of a Messiah, which of course would be a false Messiah, but their expecting him at anytime! In fact, some think he's already here! Check out these recent quotes from Jewish newspapers.

- "The most important event in the Messianic era will be the rebuilding of the Holy Temple. It is the act of building the Temple that will establish the identity of the Messiah beyond all shadow of a doubt. The Messiah will be a king over Israel, and a king can only be crowned by the Sanhedrin. The reason he will come to Jerusalem first is to be recognized by the Sanhedrin."

- "Chief Rabbi Berel Lazar believes the Earth will soon see the coming a Messiah to judge all mankind. 'We know that he is very near at hand. The Messiah may well have been born already. The world today is in a state described by our sages as 'hevley mashiah,' that is, labor that precedes the coming of a Messiah. We are living on the verge of history. It can be felt everywhere.'"

- "Rabbi Yitzchak Kaduri called upon worldwide Jewry to return to Israel due to natural disasters, which threaten to strike the world. 'In the future, the Holy One, Blessed be He, will bring about great disasters in the countries of the world to sweeten the judgments of the Land of Israel. I am ordering the publication of this declaration as a warning, so that Jews in the countries of the world will be aware of the impending danger and will come to the Land of Israel for the building of the Temple and revelation of our righteous Mashiach (Messiah). The Mashiach is already in Israel."[12]

So let's put these pieces together. The Jewish people are poised to build the end-times Temple **right now**, which might eventually include making a seven-year peace treaty with the antichrist which just so happens to be the single prophetic event that starts the clock for the seven-year Tribulation. Then we see how the Jewish people **right now** also have the means to purify the Temple, which must be in existence during the Tribulation. Then we see the rebirth of the Jewish Sanhedrin and the people's expectation that the Messiah is either coming shortly or may already be here **right now**. Therefore, the question we need to **right now** be asking ourselves is this, "How much closer is the rapture of the Church, which takes place **before** the Tribulation begins?"

Yet, even with all this amazing evidence pointing to the signs of Christ's soon return, some people still refuse to heed the warning and are headed for certain destruction, like this guy:

"Two local Pastors were fishing on the side of the road one day, and being Christians and all, they decided to make a sign that said, 'The End is Near! Turn yourself around now before it's too late!' and showed this sign to each passing car.

Well, one driver that drove by didn't appreciate the sign at all. So he shouted at them, 'Leave us alone you religious nuts!' and he kept on driving.

Then all of a sudden there was a big splash, so they looked at each other, and the one Pastor said to the other, "Do you think we should've just put up a sign that says, 'The bridge is out?'"[13]

Now, that guy didn't want to listen to the warning did he? In fact, he thought that the people who were saying it were a bunch of wackos. And yet the Bible says that this skeptical attitude would be commonplace in the end times.

2 Peter 3:3-4 "First, I want to remind you that in the last days there will be scoffers who will laugh at the truth and do every evil thing they desire. This will be their argument: 'Jesus promised to come back, did he? Then where is he? Why, as far back as anyone can remember, everything has remained exactly the same since the world was first created.'" (NLT)

People of God, I hope you're not one of those **scoffers** who wake up one day and realize too late that you've been left behind. And you know what? So does God. Because He loves you and I, He has given us the warning sign of **The Jewish People** to show us that the Tribulation could be near and Christ's 2nd Coming is rapidly approaching. Jesus Himself said this:

Luke 21:28 "When these things begin to take place, stand up and lift up your heads, because your redemption is drawing near." (NIV)

Like it or not folks, we are headed for **The Final Countdown**. We don't know the day or the hour. Only God knows. The point is, if you're a Christian, it's time to get serious and motivated about who we are and what we're called to do as Christians. Folks, it's high time we Christians speak up and declare the good news of salvation to those who are dying all around us. But please, if you're not a Christian, give your life to Jesus today, because tomorrow may be too late! Just like the Bible said!

Study Questions

- What did Pastor Billy say would be "the ultimate sign" that you're headed for the worst day of your life?

Answer: When you wake up one morning only to realize that

_____ _____ _____

_____ ..... that millions of people all over the globe are

_____ ..."that you've been _____

_____ ...

- What is coming upon this wicked and rebellious planet?

Answer: An outpouring of _____   _____

- But because God loves you and me, "He has given us many

_____ _____ that the Tribulation could

be near and Christ's 2nd Coming is rapidly approaching."

- How many signs will Pastor Billy share with us in his series "The Final Countdown"? _____

The Sermon Unfolded

The #10 sign on the final countdown is none other than _____

_____   _____ . These are specific events that

the Lord prophesied would happen to Israel.

THE 1ST END TIME PROPHECY IS THAT ISRAEL WOULD

_____ **TO THE LAND.**

Isaiah 43:5-6, Do not be afraid, for I am with you; I will bring your children from the east and gather you from the west. I will say to the north, 'Give them up!' and to the south, 'Do not hold them back.' Bring my sons from afar and my daughters from the ends of the earth—

- What has happened in the last century alone?

Answer: Millions of Jews have _____ ____ _____

_____

THE 2ND END TIME PROPHECY IS THAT ISRAEL WOULD

BECOME A _____ **AGAIN.**

Isaiah 11:11-12 In that day the Lord will reach out his hand a second time to reclaim the remnant that is left of his people from Assyria, from Lower Egypt, from Upper Egypt, from Cush, from Elam, from Babylonia, from Hamath and from the islands of the sea. He will raise a banner for the nations and gather the exiles of Israel; he will assemble the scattered people of Judah from the four quarters of the earth.

- On what date did Israel become a nation again?

Answer: _____

- What happened in 1967?

Answer: The Jewish people even _____ the city of

_____

THE 3RD END TIME PROPHECY IS THAT ISRAEL WOULD BE

_____ _____ **IN**

ONE DAY.

Isaiah 66:8, Who has ever heard of such a thing? Who has ever seen such things? Can a country be born in a day or a nation be brought forth in a moment? Yet no sooner is Zion in labor than she gives birth to her children.

- What was that important date again?

Answer: _____

THE 4TH END TIME PROPHECY IS THAT ISRAEL WOULD BE A

_____ _____**AGAIN.**

Ezekiel 37:21,22, And say to them, 'This is what the Sovereign Lord says: I will take the Israelites out of the nations where they have gone. I will gather them from all around and bring them back into their own land. I will make them one nation in the land, on the mountains of Israel. There will be one king over all of them and they will never again be two nations or be divided into two kingdoms.

- For how long had Israel been divided?

Answer: Since about _____ BC for

_____ years.

THE 5ᵀᴴ END TIME PROPHECY IS THAT ISRAEL'S

_____

WOULD BE THE _____.

Ezekiel 45:12,13,16 The shekel is to consist of twenty gerahs. Twenty shekels plus twenty-five shekels plus fifteen shekels equal one mina. This is the special gift you are to offer: a sixth of an ephah from each homer of wheat and a sixth of an ephah from each homer of barley. All the people of the land will participate in this special gift for the use of the prince in Israel.

- Israel's currency used to be "the pound"; but on what month and year did

  it change to the shekel"? _____

THE 6ᵀᴴ END TIME PROPHECY IS THAT ISRAEL WOULD

_____ AS A _____ IN THE

DESERT.

Isaiah 35:1-2; The desert and the parched land will be glad; the wilderness will rejoice and blossom. Like the crocus, it will burst into bloom; it will rejoice greatly and shout for joy. The glory of Lebanon will be given to it, the splendor of Carmel and Sharon; they will see the glory of the Lord, the splendor of our God.

- When Mark Twain visited Israel in the 1860's, what did he report?

Answer: "That Israel was a _____ _____

with no _____."

- How many trees exist in Israel today? "Over _____

_____"

- Along with ornamental plants, what else is being exported all over the

world?

Answer: An _____ of _____

THE 7TH END TIME PROPHECY IS THAT ISRAEL WOULD HAVE

A _____ _____.

Zechariah 12:6, On that day I will make the leaders of Judah like a firepot in a woodpile, like a flaming torch among sheaves. They will consume right and left all the surrounding peoples, but Jerusalem will remain intact in her place.

- What nations invaded Israel within hours after their declaration of

independence in 1948?

Answer: _____, _____, _____,

_____, and _____. The Jews won the war

and expanded their size "by _____ percent"

> # THE 8TH END TIME PROPHECY IS THAT ISRAEL WOULD BE A
>
> _____ OF _____ TO THE
>
> **WHOLE WORLD.**

Zechariah 12:2-3, I am going to make Jerusalem a cup that sends all the surrounding peoples reeling. Judah will be besieged as well as Jerusalem. On that day, when all the nations of the earth are gathered against her, I will make Jerusalem an immovable rock for all the nations. All who try to move it will injure themselves.

Israel's location in the heart of the world's _____

_____ makes it a great strategic significance to all the

countries in the world.

- Where do the three largest religions have their headquarters?

Answer: _____   _____

> # THE 9TH END TIME PROPHECY IS THAT ISRAEL WOULD
>
> _____ THE _____

Revelation 11:2, But exclude the outer court; do not measure it, because it has been given to the Gentiles. They will trample on the holy city for 42 months.

Daniel 9:27, He will confirm a covenant with many for one 'seven.' In the middle of the 'seven' he will put an end to sacrifice and offering. And on a wing of the temple he will set up an abomination that causes desolation, until the end that is decreed is poured out on him.

The Muslim Dome of the Rock has been a source of contention concerning the new proposed temple site.

- What are Jewish archaeologists saying about the actual site for the temple?

Answer: Not where the Dome of the Rock is, "but rather to the_____

or the _____ of it"

There's a group in Israel called the "Temple Institute". What are they doing at the present time?

Answer: _____ priests to serve in the _____ _____

- Everything is almost in place, with the exception of one item. What is that?

Answer: A _____ _____.

The ashes of this animal are needed for cleansing.

Numbers 19:1-4, The Lord said to Moses and Aaron: This is a requirement of the law that the Lord has commanded: Tell the Israelites to bring you a red heifer without defect or blemish and that has never been under a yoke. Give it to Eleazar the priest; it is to be taken outside the camp and slaughtered in his presence. Then Eleazar the priest is to take some of its blood on his finger and sprinkle it seven times toward the front of the Tent of Meeting.

- Even though the red heifer born in Israel a few years ago was disqualified, how could one be created?

Answer: _____ through genetic _____ and

_____

- What is Rabbi Yitzchak Kaduir calling the Jews all over the world to do?

Answer: Come to the Land of Israel for the _____ of the

Temple and revelation of our righteous_____.

Write out in full Luke 21:28

_____

_____

_____

_____

Are you ready for Jesus Christ's 2nd Coming?

Chapter Two

Modern Technology

"One day, an English businesswoman explained to her doctor that she was always breaking wind. At board meetings, during interviews, in lifts and on trams. It was impossible to control.

Then she told her doctor, 'But at least I'm fortunate in two respects: they neither smell nor make a noise. In fact, you'll be surprised to know that I've let two go since I've been talking to you.'

Well, at this the doctor reached for his pad, scribbled a prescription, and handed it to her.

'What's this for?' she asked reading the prescription. 'Nasal drops?'

'Yes,' replied the doctor. 'First we'll fix your nose, then we'll work on your hearing.'"[1]

Now that lady was in for a big surprise wasn't she? She thought everything was just fine when in reality she had some serious problems. But unfortunately, she's not alone. You see, many people in our society today **also think** that everything in the world is just fine, when in reality they're actually headed for the **ultimate surprise**; that of being left behind. Not only that, but they will also be catapulted into the seven-year Tribulation that is coming upon the whole world.

And folks, the time of the Tribulation is not a party. It's an outpouring of God's wrath upon a wicked and rebellious planet. In fact, Jesus said in **Matthew 24** that it would be a time of greater horror than anything the world has ever seen or will ever see again. He also said that unless that time of calamity is shortened, the entire human race would be destroyed. But God is not only a God of wrath; He's a God of love as well. And **because He loves you and I**, He has given us many warning signs so that we would know when the Tribulation could be near and that Christ's 2nd Coming is rapidly approaching. Therefore, to keep you and I from experiencing the ultimate surprise of being left behind, we're going to continue taking a look at **The Final Countdown**.

In the last chapter we looked at the **#10** sign on **The Final Countdown**, which was **The Jewish People**. And there we saw that God lovingly foretold you and I that when we see the Jewish people returning to the land, becoming a single united nation with a powerful military, blossoming as a rose in the desert with a currency of the shekel and preparing to rebuild the temple, that this would be an indicator that we are in the last days.

But that's not the only sign that God has given us. The **#9** sign on **The Final Countdown** is none other than **Modern Technology**. So just what are these specific prophesies being fulfilled today concerning **Modern Technology**, revealing that we could be in the last days? Well, I'm glad you asked. The **1st End Time Prophecy** concerning **Modern Technology** is that **There Would Be A Great Increase of Travel and Knowledge**.

Daniel 12:4 "But you, Daniel, keep this prophecy a secret; seal up the book until the time of the end. Many will rush here and there, and knowledge will increase." (NLT)

Many scholars see this passage as **strictly** referring to people rushing here and there, **increasing their knowledge of prophecy** in the last days. Which is exactly what we see today, do we not? Then there are those who see this passage **strictly** referring to people **traveling all over the earth** with an **explosion of information like never before**. Which is **also** exactly what we see today, do we not? Therefore, I think that it's not necessarily one or the other, **but actually both**.

So, specifically, just what kind of **Modern Technology** has arisen to enable this prophecy to come to pass? Well, I'm glad you asked. The **1st** way that **Modern Technology** reveals that we could be in the last days is by an **Increase of Travel**. You see, when Daniel wrote down the words of this prophecy, the mode of travel had been basically the same for thousands of years. It's only **in this last century alone** that we've seen a major change in transportation.

For instance, the fastest that mankind could travel for thousands of years was about 30 mph via horseback. From Adam to Alexander the Great to Abraham Lincoln, transportation pretty much stayed the same.[2] For instance, at the turn of the century in New York, the major traffic concern was **dead horses**! Each year there were about 15,000 horses dying from exhaustion, beatings, or accidents. And believe it or not, they had their own air pollution too. How's that you say? Well, only from a **million pounds** of manure produced every day! That's right, people quickly learned to keep their windows closed during the summer. But by and large, the major means of transportation for thousands of years was the horse.[3]

That is, until now. **All in the last century alone**, we have gone from the horse to the horseless carriage; the car. We've gone from a top speed of 30 mph to literally hundreds of mph. And in **just a few decades**, we now **rush here and**

there an average of 14,000 miles per year, with an estimated **1 Billion** cars on the road by 2025.[4]

Oh, but that's only by land. Thanks to the invention of the airplane, **which also occurred in the last century**, the world has become a much smaller place. For instance, the first flight by the Wright brothers was only 120 feet. Had they flown from the back of a Boeing 747 they wouldn't have even made it to first class. The first plane had limited seating. But a Boeing 747 can carry more than 400 passengers, fly 8,300 miles without refueling, has 6 million parts, 171 miles of wiring, 5 miles of tubing, and a tail the size of a six-story building.[5]

And because there are so many people traveling today, the industry is making it even easier and faster to **rush here and there**, just like the Bible said would happen. For instance, you can not only order your tickets online, but also print boarding passes from your own computer. And for those of you who worry about your loved ones flying, **worry no more**. Thanks to the Internet, you can follow a flight in transit, graphics and all, observe the speed and altitude it's traveling, and be told when it has arrived.[6]

Oh, but that's not all. Because of this new travel technology, you can go down to your local store and get fresh crabmeat from Thailand, or have a thoroughbred horse shipped to you from New Zealand. You can now get fresh flowers from South America, a genuine New York City pizza delivered anywhere in the world, and send a package from Japan in the afternoon and have it in Washington by the next morning.[7]

Oh, but the friendly skies are not the only place we like to **rush here and there**. You see, the airplane paved the way for **space travel**. Now we can fly around the planet in eighty minutes.[8] We not only went to the moon and back, but now our eyes are on the planet Mars. And people, keep in mind that this is **in**

the last century alone! Do you get the feeling that things are being sped up? Somehow, Star Trek doesn't sound so foreign anymore, does it? Speaking of which, did you know that **teleportation is no longer a myth**? That's right, in the past couple of years, scientists have successfully teleported light particles over a few miles.[9] It would appear as if nothing is holding us back from being able to **rush here and there**, wherever and whenever we want.

That is, except God. You see, the sad thing is that this explosion of modern travel technology has made us arrogant and overconfident like the Edomites of long ago **who also tried to escape** the boundaries of Almighty God. **Obadiah 1:3-4** "The arrogance of your heart has deceived you, You who live in the clefts of the rock, In the loftiness of your dwelling place, Who say in your heart, Who will bring me down to earth?' Though you build high like the eagle, Though you set your nest among the stars, From there I will bring you down," declares the LORD." (NAS)

You see, even if we can one day **arrogantly boast** that we don't need God because we can **rush here and there**, even to the edge of the stars, God will one day, just like the Edomites, bring us down. When? In the last days.

The **2nd** way that **Modern Technology** reveals that we could be in the last days is by an **Increase of Knowledge**. When Daniel wrote down the words of this prophecy, the amount of retrieving and sharing knowledge was severely limited. We didn't even see the invention of the printing press until a few centuries ago. Oh, but look at us today! **All in the last century alone**, just like the Bible said, we are experiencing nothing short of an information explosion! In fact, let's take a look at some information on information:

1. The total store of human knowledge is now doubling every 8 years.
2. 80% of all the scientists who have ever lived are alive today.
3. Every minute 2000 pages are added to man's scientific knowledge.
4. The scientific material produced in 1 day would take 1 person 5 years to read.

5. About 1/2 million new books are published every year.
6. Since 1970 computer technology has developed so fast that if the auto industry had developed at the same rate, you would today be able to buy a Rolls Royce for three dollars and you could fit 8 them on the head of a pin!
7. A weekday edition of any major newspaper has more information than the average person living in the 17th century would have come across in a lifetime.
8. Thanks to the Internet, 1,000's of international papers are at your fingertips.
9. Every day, the equivalent of over 300 million pages of text is sent over the Internet with millions of sites.
10. About 1/2 of all medical knowledge is outdated every 10 years and in some scientific fields, such as biotechnology, the cycle is less than 6 months.
11. There are now wristwatches that wield more computing ability than some 1970s computer mainframes.
12. Ordinary cars today have more intelligence than the original lunar lander.
13. The majority of the world either has a television or access to one.[10]

And speaking of the advent of worldwide television, **in the last century alone**, we can see **for the first time** the fulfillment of this passage of Scripture concerning the death of God's faithful two witnesses during the Tribulation.

Revelation 11:9-10 "For three and a half days men from every people, tribe, language and nation will gaze on their bodies and refuse them burial. The inhabitants of the earth will gloat over them and will celebrate by sending each other gifts, because these two prophets had tormented those who live on the earth." (NIV)

Now imagine when the Apostle John was writing this. It must have seemed like an incredible fantasy **for the whole planet** to simultaneously watch two dead bodies, rejoice over their death, and even send gifts to each other. That is, **until now**. Due to the advent of television and global satellite technology, you and I can **simultaneously** watch anything we want, can't we? And now with the

Internet, we can even send gifts to **literally anyone** on the planet at anytime. Just like the Bible said! When? In the last days.

The **3rd** way that **Modern Technology** reveals that we could be in the last days is by an **Increase of Unrest**.

2 Timothy 3:1,7 "But mark this: There will be terrible times in the last days. Always learning but never able to acknowledge the truth." (NIV)

You see, the Bible also warned that in the last days, not only would we be traveling like never before and acquiring information like crazy, but we would also **see an increase of unrest**. Why? Because we would become a people who are always learning yet are never able to acknowledge the truth, leaving us in a frustrated and restless state. And folks, is this not exactly what has happened to our society? We are being told today that the more we acquire this **new technology**, the more time it will save us, so we can spend even more time **rushing here and there**. Then, if that wasn't bad enough, we are being told that the more we can learn from this **increase of information**, the more peace it will supposedly produce in our lives.

But is this true? Have we really saved more time and created more peace in our lives with all this new technology? Absolutely not! We have actually become a society on the brink of disaster! And this is exactly what the **secular experts** are saying. Even though we have the most highly funded educational system in the world, we are producing the most confused, ignorant and violent children ever.[11] Rates of depression have been doubling every ten years and suicide is the third most common cause of death among young adults in North America. Fifteen percent of Americans have had a clinical anxiety disorder and serial killers are now commonplace.[12]

How can this be? It's simply because we are always learning yet never able to come to the truth! You see, **the truth is** that the more we fill our lives with so-called timesaving devices, the more rushed we feel. In fact, we are in so much of a rush that "we tap our fingers while waiting for the microwave to zap our instant coffee."[13] Think about it! **The truth is**, these devices that are supposed to save us so much time so that we can rest more, are actually making us **more restless**. In fact, one researcher made this comment. See if it sounds familiar:

"This century's mad dash of innovation has produced the most frantic human era ever. We phone. We fax. We page. We e-mail. We race from one end of life to the other, rarely glancing over our shoulders. Technology, mass media and a desire to do more, do it better and do it yesterday have turned us into a world of hurriers. Stop and smell the roses? No more. Instead, we have a world of 7-day diets, 24-hour news channels, 1-hour photo, 30-minute pizza delivery, 10-minute facials, 2-minute warnings, and Minute Rice. Fast food. Fast computers. Fast cars in fast lanes. VCRs with 5 fast-forward settings. Sound bites and the rat race and instant coffee. Get rich quick. Live fast, die young, leave a good-looking corpse. Run on empty. Just do it. Places to go, people to meet, planners to fill, files to download, bills to pay, planes to catch, frozen dinners to nuke, web sites to surf, kids to pick up, stress to manage, and speeding tickets to pay."[14]

One guy said, "It's significant that we call it the Information Age. We don't talk about the Knowledge Age. Our society is basically motion without memory, which of course is one of the clinical definitions of **insanity**."[15]

We have advanced beyond our wildest dreams technologically, yet we are still spiritually bankrupt about the **true meaning of life**. And it's all because we have been tricked and seduced by a **restless** rat race society!

You see, the problem of being in a **hurry all the time** is that you never take the time to stop and think about what is most important in life. Therefore, you will never find the truth. And that's exactly what the devil is up to.

"One day the devil called a worldwide convention of his evil demons and said this. 'We can't keep the Christians from going to heaven, but we can keep them from forming an intimate relationship in Christ. If they gain that connection with Jesus, our power over them is broken. So here's what we do

Let's steal their time, so they can't gain any strength in Jesus Christ. Let's distract them by keeping them busy in the nonessentials of life and invent unnumbered schemes to occupy their minds. We'll over stimulate their minds so that they cannot hear that still small voice.

We'll entice them to play the radio or cassette player whenever they drive, to keep the TV, the VCR, and their CD's going constantly in their homes. And we'll see to it that every store and restaurant in the world plays music constantly jamming their minds to break that union with Christ.

We'll fill their coffee tables with magazines and newspapers and pound their minds with the news twenty-four hours a day. We'll invade their driving moments with billboards and flood their mailboxes with junk mail, sweepstakes, mail order catalogues and every kind of newsletter and promotional offering promising false hopes.

We'll even get them to be excessive in their entertainment or recreation and send them to amusement parks, sporting events, concerts, and movies so they'll return exhausted, disquieted and unprepared for the coming week.

And even when they meet for spiritual fellowship, we'll involve them in gossip and small talk so that they leave with troubled consciences and unsettled emotion. Why, we'll crowd their lives with **so many things** that they have no time or energy to seek power from Christ.

It was quite a convention in the end. And the demons went away eagerly causing Christians everywhere to get busy, busy, busy and rush here and there. Don't forget what 'busy' means. B-eing U-nder S-atan's Y-oke. Has the devil been successful at his scheme? You be the judge."[16]

I'll say it one last time. The problem of being in a **hurry all the time** is that you never take the time to stop and think about that which is the most important in life. And because of that, it's not only a sign that you're living in the last days, but that you've been lassoed by satan's yoke and therefore, you will never find the truth because you're just too busy! Wake up! Instead of worshipping the one True God, we have **bowed to the idol of technology**. And the sad thing is that the truth about life is right before us, if only we'd stop long enough to listen. You see, we don't need to travel halfway across the world for truth. In fact, we don't even need that latest computer gizmo to understand it, nor spend a dime to receive it. Why? Because the truth about a **restful life** has been right under our noses all the time, in the words of Jesus Christ.

Matthew 11:28 "Then Jesus said, 'Come to me, all of you who are weary and carry heavy burdens, and I will give you rest.'" (NLT)

People of God, please don't be fooled into thinking that by **rushing here and there** and by **increasing your knowledge** is where you'll find rest. Because if you do, you will not only remain restless, but you may one day wake up to find yourself in the **greatest time of unrest** the world has ever known, the Great Tribulation. Just like the Bible said. When? In the last days.

And believe it or not, even with all this amazing evidence pointing to the signs of Christ's soon return, some people still refuse to admit the truth and are in certain danger, like these people:

"One day a group of Florida senior citizens were sitting around talking about their ailments when one person said, 'My arms are so weak I can hardly hold this cup of coffee.'

'Yes, I know.' Replied another. 'My cataracts are so bad I can't even see my coffee.'

Then the person with the loudest voice of the group piped in, 'Oh yeah, well it's gotten to where I cannot hear anything anymore.'

Then a fourth person nodded weakly in agreement, 'I know what you mean, I can't turn my head because of the arthritis in my neck.'

'Well, that's nothing,' claimed another 'my blood pressure pills make me dizzy.'

'You think that's bad," said another person, 'Why I can't even remember what I'm doing half the time. If I don't make myself a note I forget what I am trying to do in the first place.'

Then an old wise man of the group winced and shook his head saying, 'I guess that's the price we pay for getting old.'

Then there was a short moment of silence and one woman cheerfully announced, 'Well, it's not that bad. Thank goodness we can all still drive.'"[17]

Now those people didn't want to admit the truth, did they? And because of this they were not only a danger to themselves but to other people as well. And yet the Bible says that this refusal to admit the truth would be commonplace in the last days, just like it was with Noah.

Matthew 24:37-39 "When the Son of Man returns, it will be like it was in Noah's day. In those days before the Flood, the people were enjoying banquets and parties and weddings right up to the time Noah entered his boat. People didn't realize what was going to happen until the Flood came and swept them all away. That is the way it will be when the Son of Man comes." (NLT)

People of God, I hope you're not one of those who are too busy partying and acting like nothing will ever change. Because if you are, you might wake up one day and discover that **you've been left behind**. And you know what? God doesn't want you left behind. Because He loves you and I, He has given us the warning sign of **Modern Technology** to show us that the Tribulation **could be near** and that Christ's 2nd Coming is rapidly approaching. Jesus Himself said this:

Luke 21:28 "When these things begin to take place, stand up and lift up your heads, because your redemption is drawing near." (NIV)

Like it or not folks, we are headed for **The Final Countdown**. We don't know the day or the hour. Only God knows. The point is, if you're a Christian, it's time to get busy. There's a war going on and each of us needs to find something to do to serve the Lord while we still can. Folks, it's high time we Christians speak up and declare the good news of salvation to those who are dying all around us. But please, if you're not a Christian, give your life to Jesus today, because tomorrow may be too late! Just like the Bible said!

Study Questions

Review

The first chapter in this book dealt with Sign #10 that shows that Christ's Coming is right around the corner.

- What was that sign?

Answer: _____ _____ _____

Point of Discussion

What can you remember about the Jewish people in the end times?

This Chapter

- What is sign #9 that we're in the last days of the final countdown before Jesus' Coming?

Answer: _____ _____

THE 1ST END TIME PROPHECY CONCERNING MODERN TECHNOLOGY IS THAT THERE WOULD BE A GREAT INCREASE OF _____.

Daniel 12:4 "But you, Daniel, close up and seal the words of the scroll until the time of the end. *Many will rush here and there*."

"It's only this last century alone that we've seen a major change in transportation."

- How did people travel for thousands of years?

Answer: via _____.

- What is the present avenue of travel on land and what is the average miles per year that we travel?

Answer: The _____ and _____ miles per year.

In the air, travel has also greatly increased. Put down some statistics concerning a Boeing 747:

- Can carry more than _____ passengers.
- Can fly _____ miles without refueling.
- Has _____ million parts.
- _____ miles of wiring.

- _____miles of tubing.

- A tail the size of a _____ building.

Now we're traveling in outer space. We have space craft that can fly around our planet in _____ minutes.

- What is no longer a myth?

Answer: _____

Scientists have successfully teleported light particles over a few miles.

- Who is the only one who can hold us back from rushing here and there?

Answer: _____

- But what has this travel explosiveness produced in us?

Answer: Has made us _____ and _____ like the Edomites of long ago…

Obadiah 1:3-4 "The arrogance of your heart has deceived you, You who live in the clefts of the rock, In the loftiness of your dwelling place, who say in your heart, Who will bring me down to earth?" Though you build high like the eagle, though you set your nest among the stars, From there I will bring you down," declares the LORD.

THE 2ND END TIME PROPHECY CONCERNING MODERN

TECHNOLOGY IS THAT THERE WOULD BE A GREAT

_____ _____.

Daniel 12:4 "But you, Daniel, close up and seal the words of the scroll until the time of the end. Many will go here and there and **knowledge will increase**."

As Pastor Billy shares 13 proofs that there has been a gigantic explosion of knowledge with the last century, list as many as you can.

1.

2.

3.

4.

5.

6.

7.

8.

9.

10.

11.

12.

13.

- What two media avenues are reaching people all over the world?

Answer: _____ and the _____

This might explain how the three and a half days prophecy of the two witnesses

in the following verse:

Revelation 11:9-10, "For three and a half days **men from every people, tribe, language and nation will gaze on their bodies** and refuse them burial. The inhabitants of the earth **will gloat over them and will celebrate by sending each other gifts**, because these two prophets had tormented those who live on the earth."

THE 3RD END TIME PROPHECY AS IT CONCERNS MODERN

TECHNOLOGY IS THAT THERE WILL BE A GREAT INCREASE

OF _____.

---

2 Timothy 3:1,7 "But mark this: There will be terrible times in the last days. Always learning but never able to acknowledge the truth."

Point of Discussion

- Even though we have the most highly funded educational system in the

world", what are we producing?

Answer: The most _____ _____and _____

children ever. Always learning and yet never able to come to the truth.

Why do you think all the modern technology could cause people a lot of unrest?

Rates of depression have been doubling every _____ years. _____is

the third most common cause of death among young adults in North America.

_____ _____ are now commonplace."

- What happens "the more we fill our lives with so-called timesaving

    devices"?

Answer: "The more _____ we feel.

One researcher had this to say:

"This century's mad dash of innovation has produced the most _____,

_____ _____ ever."

Our society is basically _____ without _____, which of

course is one of the clinical definitions of _____."

- For many Christians, all over the world, what does the acrostic BUSY

    mean?   B – _____

                          U – _____

                          S – _____

                          Y – _____

Point of Discussion: Can you think of any ways that we could be in bondage to satan's hold?

- What is the only truth that can set us free?

Answer: Matthew 11:28, which reads, "Come to me, all you who are weary and burdened, and I will give you rest.

Have you entered God's place of rest, Jesus Christ? You need to make sure!

God is counting down the moments before His Son's return. How? With the signs that He has given us that Jesus is coming soon.

What did Jesus, Himself say in Luke 21:28? "When these things begin to take place, stand up and lift up your heads, because your redemption is drawing near."

It is drawing near my friend.   Be ready to meet Him before it's too late!

Are you ready for Jesus Christ's 2nd Coming?

Chapter Three

Worldwide Upheaval

Hey, how many of you men out there enjoy summertime? I like it because it's a great time to express our **manliness**. How's that? Well, need you ask? Summertime equals BBQ time! And what better way to express your manliness than to be around a roaring flame and a pile of meat, huh? But I've noticed that BBQ's are not only a good time to declare to the world our masculinity, they're actually a great time to help our wives as well. How's that? By offering to cook supper once in awhile via a BBQ, we not only score points by being manly, but we also get to help around the house at the same time. And because it is so important for us husbands to help our wives out as much as we can, I want to make sure we are all on the same page here; especially those of you who might be new to the "BBQ thing." We're going to look at some surefire steps to a successful BBQ. Ladies, see if these steps sound familiar to you:

1. The woman goes to the store.
2. The woman fixes the salad, vegetables, and dessert.
3. The woman prepares the meat for cooking, places it on a tray along with the necessary cooking utensils, and takes it to the man, who is lounging beside the grill.

4. The man places the meat on the grill.
5. The woman goes inside to set the table and check the vegetables.
6. The woman comes out to tell the man that the meat is burning.
7. The man takes the meat off the grill and hands it to the woman.
8. The woman prepares the plates and brings them to the table.
9. After eating, the woman clears the table and does the dishes.
10. The man now asks the woman how she enjoyed "her night off," and upon seeing her annoyed reaction, concludes that there's just no pleasing some women.[1]

Yes, men, it's very hard pleasing our wives; no matter how hard we try, isn't it? Go figure. But guys, don't feel too bad. Nobody can please everybody all the time. And that's not only with the BBQ but with the Bible as well. You see, three-quarters of the Bible deals directly or indirectly with prophetic issues and therefore needs to be addressed. And you'd think that people would rejoice over being able to know what lies ahead in the future. Yet, unfortunately, many people are actually **displeased** to find out that the world is going to get worse before it gets better and that we'd better get ready. And because they don't want to hear it and receive Christ as their Savior, they are running the risk of being left behind. They will be catapulted into the seven-year Tribulation that is coming upon the whole world.

And folks, the time of the Tribulation is not a party. It's an outpouring of God's wrath upon a wicked and rebellious planet. In fact Jesus said in **Matthew 24** that it would be a time of greater horror than anything the world has ever seen or will ever see again. He also said that unless that time of calamity is shortened, the entire human race would be destroyed. But God is not only a God of wrath; He's a God of love as well. And **because He loves you and I**, He has given us many warning signs so that we would know when the Tribulation could be near and that Christ's 2nd Coming is rapidly approaching. Therefore, to keep us from being severely displeased from being left behind, we're going to continue taking a look at **The Final Countdown**.

We already saw the **#10** sign on **The Final Countdown**, which was **The Jewish People**. And in the last chapter we saw that the **#9** sign was none other then **Modern Technology**. There we saw that God lovingly foretold you and I that when we see an increase of travel, an increase of information, and an increase of unrest, that this would be an indicator that we are in the last days. But that's not the only signs that God has given us.

The **#8** sign on **The Final Countdown** is none other than **Worldwide Upheaval**. So just what are these specific prophesies being fulfilled today concerning **Worldwide Upheaval**, revealing that we could be in the last days? Well, I'm glad you asked. Let's take a look.

Matthew 24:1-8 "Jesus left the temple and was walking away when His disciples came up to Him to call His attention to its buildings. Do you see all these things? He asked. I tell you the truth, not one stone here will be left on another; every one will be thrown down. As Jesus was sitting on the Mount of Olives, the disciples came to Him privately. Tell us, they said, when will this happen, and what will be the sign of Your coming and of the end of the age?

Jesus answered: Watch out that no one deceives you. For many will come in My name, claiming, I am the Christ, and will deceive many. You will hear of wars and rumors of wars, but see to it that you are not alarmed. Such things must happen, but the end is still to come. Nation will rise against nation, and kingdom against kingdom. There will be famines and earthquakes in various places. All these are the beginning of birth pains." (NIV)

According to our text there, one of the signs to indicate that we are headed for **Worldwide Upheaval** is that there would be an **Increase of Earthquakes**. Now the scoffer would look at this passage and sarcastically state, "Earthquakes are no big deal, we've always had earthquakes." And yes, that is true, except for the last century. **In the last century alone**, we have seen nothing short of an explosion of **worldwide earthquakes** like never before. Here, see for yourself:

EARTHQUAKES 6.0 OR GREATER

From 1000 AD to 1800	21	(800 Years)
From 1800 to 1900	18	(100 Years)
From 1910 to 1929	4	(20 Years)
From 1930 to 1949	9	(20 Years)
In 1950's	9	(10 Years)
In 1960's	13	(10 Years)
In 1970's	51	(10 Years)
In 1980's	86	(10 Years)
From 1990 to 1994	Over 100	(5 Years)

EARTHQUAKES IN GENERAL

December 26th, 2006	454	(1 Week just in the U.S.)
February 13th, 2008	1,100	(1 Week just in the U.S.)[2]

I think it's pretty obvious that earthquakes are seriously on the rise. What do you think? Now keep in mind that although earthquakes last for a few seconds or minutes, **the trail of devastation lasts a long time**. For instance, because of this massive rise of earthquakes, they produce **billions** of dollars worth of damage, they kill **thousands** of people (one quake alone killed 17,000)[3] and they make **hundreds of thousands** of people homeless **each year**. Oh, and it's only getting worse. This sudden "increase of severe earthquakes have led scientists to

predict that **we are entering a new period of great seismic disturbances.**"[4]
Hmmm, where have I heard that before? Also, they are predicting that the death
toll from earthquakes are only going to **skyrocket** due to the massive exodus of
people who are moving out of the rural areas and into the big cities. And the
problem with this is that many of the cities just happen to be built right on top of
fault lines. Therefore, scientists are now saying that we are entering a time when
fatalities from earthquakes totaling over **one million will not be uncommon.**[5]
As you guys can see, the world is being **shaken** like never before. Yes, we may
have always had earthquakes, **but nothing like we see today**. Just like the Bible
said. When? In the last days.

The **2nd** sign to indicate that we are headed for **Worldwide Upheaval** is
that there would be an **Increase of Famines**.

Matthew 24:3,7,8 "As Jesus was sitting on the Mount of Olives, the disciples
came to him privately. Tell us, they said, when will this happen, and what will be
the sign of your coming and of the end of the age? There will be famines and
earthquakes in various places. All these are the beginning of birth pains." (NIV)

Now the scoffer would look at this passage and sarcastically state,
"Famines are no big deal, we've always had famines." And yes, that is true,
except for the last century. **In the last century alone**, we have seen nothing short
of an explosion of **worldwide famines** like never before. The World Health
Organization estimates that while one-third of the world is well-fed, another one-
third is under-fed and the final one-third **is starving to death right now**. Just in
the 1990's alone, **one hundred million** children starved to death. A total of **four
million people** will die from starvation this year alone. And this means that by
about the time you finish reading this chapter, another **two hundred people** will
have died due to food shortages.[6]

But the question is, how can there be such an increase of worldwide famine when we are living in the most technologically advanced era ever? Well, war, embargoes, government corruption, and economic debt cause some. But it's also partly caused by overzealous environmentalists who have stirred up restrictions on the usage of fertilizers, which is one of the reasons why **12,000 square miles a year** of Africa is now turning into desert.[7] That doesn't sound like saving the earth to me! And speaking of deserts, the Africans are not the only ones with this problem. So are the Chinese. Today, as we speak, China is losing **4,000 square miles** of land to deserts each year. About one-third of their total land has now been covered by desert in the form of massive drifting sand dunes.[8] In fact, throughout the world, **a land area bigger than the state of Texas** is becoming deserts **every year**.[9] And no matter what people try to do to reverse it, the deserts just keep on coming. And so will famine. As you guys can see, the world is being **shriveled** like never before. Yes, we may have always had famines, **but nothing like we see today**. Just like the Bible said. When? In the last days.

The **3rd** sign to indicate that we are headed for **Worldwide Upheaval** is that there would be an **Increase of Pestilence**. Let's go to the parallel passage of Matthew 24 in Luke 21.

Luke 21:7,11 "Teacher, they asked, when will these things happen? And what will be the sign that they are about to take place? There will be great earthquakes, famines and pestilences in various places, and fearful events and great signs from heaven." (NIV)

Now the scoffer would look at this passage and sarcastically state, "Pestilence is no big deal, we've always had outbreaks of diseases."[10] And yes, that is true, except for the last century. **In the last century alone**, we have seen nothing short of an explosion of **worldwide pestilence** like never before. As recently as 1979, the U.S. Surgeon General made this bold announcement, "It is time to close the books on infectious diseases." Now, was he right in his prediction? I don't think so! By the 1990's, instead of fading out of existence, **infectious diseases have gone ballistic**. We've all heard of the AIDS virus, but did you know that 36 million people have it worldwide and it's growing like wildfire daily? Did you know that in 1998 the combined wars in Africa killed 200,000 people but AIDS killed **10 times more** than that?[11] Did you also know that 75% of all HIV infections are now being spread via heterosexual contact?[12] But people, AIDS isn't the half of it. Diseases that were once considered conquered such as tuberculosis, malaria, cholera, diphtheria, and even the black plague are coming back with a vengeance![13]

But the question is, how can there be such an increase of worldwide pestilence when we're living in the most medically advanced era ever? Well, other than scientific experimentation and biological warfare, it's partly **due to an overuse of antibiotics**. You see, because we have saturated ourselves with so many antibiotics, the **diseases are now mutating** and becoming resistant to all medication. And this has alarmed the medical community so much that they have stated that "the emergence of bacteria strains that cannot be killed by the current arsenal of antibiotics could become a public health threat **worse than AIDS**."[14] In fact, at a meeting of the American Association for the Advancement of Science in 1994, scientists announced that they see us heading towards, "**nothing short of a medical disaster**."[15] As you guys can see, the world is being filled with **sickness** like never before. Yes, we may have always had pestilence, **but nothing like we see today**. Just like the Bible said. When? In the last days.

The **4th** sign to indicate that we are headed for **Worldwide Upheaval** is that there would be an **Increase of Wars**.

Matthew 24:3,6,7 "As Jesus was sitting on the Mount of Olives, the disciples came to him privately. Tell us, they said, when will this happen, and what will be the sign of your coming and of the end of the age? You will hear of wars and rumors of wars…nation will rise against nation, and kingdom against kingdom." (NIV)

Now, the scoffer would look at this passage and sarcastically state, "Wars are no big deal, we've always had wars." And yes, that is true, except for the last century. **In the last century alone**, we have seen nothing short of an explosion of **worldwide wars** like never before. For instance, more people have been killed by wars in the last century than at any other time in mankind's history.[16] In fact, prior to WWI, war had never been universal. But not only have we had two of them, but after WWII, which was supposed to be the war to end all wars, there have been **more then 150 major wars**.[17] In 1993 alone there were a record of twenty-nine major wars being fought.[18] However, that record was soon to be broken because two years later in 1995 there were seventy-one.[19] In fact, the whole world is gearing up like never before for more war.

And speaking of the rise of wars and the armies that go along with them, **in the last century alone** we can see **for the first time** the possible fulfillment of this passage of Scripture concerning a 200 million man army.

Revelation 9:15-16 "And the four angels who had been prepared for this hour and day and month and year were turned loose to kill one-third of all the people on earth. They led an army of 200 million mounted troops – I heard an announcement of how many there were." (NLT)

Now some people would say that this is just referring to a demonic host of 200 million that will be released to kill one-third of mankind. And it could be. I personally don't want to be there to find out. However, with the explosion of the world population, can you guess just who it is that has gone on record **back** in the 1960's of already having a literal 200 million-man army? That's right! China.[20]

Oh, but that's not all. **In the last century alone**, we can see **for the first time**, the possible fulfillment of this passage of Scripture concerning the disintegration of human flesh to the bone while a person is still standing:

Zechariah 14:12 "This is the plague with which the Lord will strike all the nations that fought against Jerusalem: Their flesh will rot while they are still standing on their feet, their eyes will rot in their sockets, and their tongues will rot in their mouths." (NIV)

Now some people would say that this is just some sovereign act of God where He supernaturally causes a plague that instantly removes people's flesh while they're standing; and it could be. I personally don't want to be there to find out. However, with the modern weaponry that we see today, what does that graphic description sound like to you? Kind of like a nuclear holocaust, doesn't it? It might even be from a biological weapon. But either way, **in the last century alone**, we can get a good idea, can't we?

And speaking of nuclear warfare, as of the year 2000, just between the U.S. and Russia, we now have enough nuclear bombs to destroy the planet **six times over!**[21] But that's not the half of it. Even **small countries** all over the world **right now** have their own supply of nuclear weapons, and it's only increasing each year. Many already believe that it's not a matter of if, but **when and where** the first nuclear strike will be. And what happens after that, no one knows for sure. As you guys can see, the world is being **shot to pieces** like never before. Yes, we may have always had wars, **but nothing like we see today**. Just like the Bible said. When? In the last days.

And believe it or not, even with all this amazing evidence pointing to the signs of Christ's soon return, some people are still having a hard time receiving the truth, like this story reveals:

"A man goes to the White House and asks to see President Clinton.

So the Marine on duty quickly informs the guy that Bill Clinton is no longer the President, and then asked him to please leave.

So the man goes away. But the next day the same guy comes back to the White House and asks to see President Clinton again.

So the marine on duty reminds him that Clinton is not the President, and to please go away.

So the man goes away. However, the next day, the same guy comes back again, and again the same Marine is on duty.

So the man asks to see President Clinton, and at this the Marine finally lost his patience so he yells back, 'WHY DO YOU KEEP COMING HERE ASKING FOR CLINTON? BILL CLINTON IS NOT THE PRESIDENT ANYMORE!!!'"

At this the man smiles and says, 'I know, I just like hearing it.'"[22]

Now that guy just couldn't get enough of the good news, could he? But believe it or not, there are still some people out there who are still having a hard time with this news. Shocker, isn't it? And yet the Bible said that in the last days, many people will also have a hard time receiving the truth and will instead be living in a dream world acting like nothing will ever change. Just like it was in Lot's day.

Luke 17:28-30 "And the world will be as it was in the days of Lot. People went about their daily business – eating and drinking, buying and selling, farming and building – until the morning Lot left Sodom. Then fire and burning sulfur rained down from heaven and destroyed them all. Yes, it will be 'business as usual' right up to the hour when the Son of Man returns." (NLT)

People of God, I hope you're not one of those who are living your life like it's "business as usual." Why? Because if you are, you might wake up one day and discover that **you've been left behind**. And you know what? God doesn't want you left behind. Because He loves you and I, He has given us the warning sign of **Worldwide Upheaval** to show us that the Tribulation **could be near** and that Christ's 2nd Coming is rapidly approaching. Jesus Himself said this:

Luke 21:28 "When these things begin to take place, stand up and lift up your heads, because your redemption is drawing near." (NIV)

Like it or not folks, we are headed for **The Final Countdown**. We don't know the day or the hour. Only God knows. The point is, if you're a Christian, you need to realize that we are going to be dead a lot longer than we are alive. Therefore, let's not waste our lives on temporary things, but let's strive for those things that are eternal. Folks, it's high time we Christians speak up and declare the good news of salvation to those who are dying all around us. But please, if you're not a Christian, give your life to Jesus today, because tomorrow may be too late! Just like the Bible said!

Study Questions

Review

Can you remember the first two signs that Jesus' coming is very, very near?

Sign #10 is _____ _____ _____

Sign #9 is _____ _____

This Chapter:

The #8 sign on The Final Countdown is none other than _____

_____.

THE 1ST END TIME PROPHECY CONCERNING THIS SIGN OF A

WORLDWIDE UPHEAVAL IS THAT THERE WOULD BE AN

_____ _____ _____.

In Matthew 24:7 Jesus predicted, "There will be…earthquakes in various places."

In Luke 21:11 it states, "There will be _____ earthquakes…"

Jesus told us that, not only would earthquakes increase just before His Coming, but also the magnitude of these quakes would become higher on the Richter Scale; and that's exactly what has happened.

From 1000 AD through the 1950's, there were only 40 earthquakes with a magnitude of 6.0 or greater – in 959 years only 40. But what has happened in just the last 47 years plus? Record your findings with Pastor Billy.

In the 1960's there were _____ 6.0 or greater earthquakes.

In the 1970's there were _____

In the 1980's there were _____

From 1990 through 1994 (5 years), there were _____

December 26th, 2006, in just 1-week alone in the United States, there were

_____ of these earthquakes.

February 13th, 2008, in just 1-week alone in the U. S., there were _____

Not only are these huge earthquakes explosively on the rise, but the results are

devastating. Note the following that Pastor Billy shares with us:

"they produce _____ of dollars worth of damage"

"they kill _____ of people"

"they make _____ _____ _____ of people homeless"

"Scientists are now saying that we are entering a time when

_____ from earthquakes totaling over one _____

will not be uncommon."

> ## THE 2ND END TIME PROPHECY CONCERNING THIS SIGN OF A WORLDWIDE UPHEAVAL IS THAT THERE WOULD BE AN
>
> _____ _____ _____.

Jesus predicted in Matthew 24:7, "There will be famines…in various places."

The fulfillment of this prophecy from our Lord, has also exploded before our very eyes.

- What did the World Health Organization (W.H.O.) estimate concerning two-thirds of the world population?

Answer: One-third is _____ and the final one-third is

_____ _____ _____ right now.

- How many children starved to death in the 1990's alone?

Answer: _____ million

- How many people will die of starvation in this year alone?

Answer: _____ million

Pastor Billy shares some reasons for an increase in worldwide famine even though we live in the most technologically advanced era ever. List what he mentioned:

1.   _____

2.   _____

3.   _____ _____

4.   _____ _____

5. _____ _____ who have

stirred up restrictions on the usage of fertilizers, which is one of the reasons why 12,000 square miles a year of Africa is now turning into desert." With more and more desert areas comes more and more starvation.

THE 3RD END TIME PROPHECY CONCERNING THIS SIGN OF

WORLDWIDE UPHEAVAL IS THAT THERE WOULD BE AN

_____ _____ _____.

The parallel passage of Matthew 24 in Luke 21:11 reads: "There will be … pestilences in various places."

Again, this prophecy from our Lord has also been explosively fulfilled.
In 1979, the U.S. Surgeon General made a bold announcement by saying, "It is time to close the books on infectious diseases."

But actually, the opposite scenario went into effect.

- What happened by the 1990's?

Answer: Infectious diseases have gone _____.

- How many people worldwide have the AIDS virus?

Answer: _____million people

And the statistics show that it's "growing like wildfire daily."

- What other diseases are coming back with a vengeance that were once considered?

Answer: _____, _____,

_____, _____ and even the

_____ _____."

- Why has there been such an increase of worldwide pestilence?

Answer: Other than scientific _____ and biological

_____, it's partly due to an _____ of

_____.

We have saturated ourselves with so many antibiotics, the diseases are now

_____ and becoming _____ to all medications.

> # THE 4TH END TIME PROPHECY CONCERNING THE SIGN OF
>
> ## WORLDWIDE UPHEAVAL IS THAT THERE WOULD BE AN
>
> _____ _____ _____.

Our Lord also predicted in Matthew 24:7, "Nation will rise against nation, and kingdom against kingdom."

- What was true prior to World War I?

Answer: War had never been _____.

- How many "major wars" have been fought since W.W. II?

Answer: More than _____.

Record how many major wars there were in:

1993 → _____

1995 → _____

Revelation 9:15-16, "And the four angels who had been prepared for this hour and day and month and year were turned loose to kill one-third of all the people on earth. They led an army of 200 million mounted troops – I heard an announcement of how many there were."

The possibility of this fulfillment, of a _____ million-man army is on the horizon.

- Back in the 1960's, what country went on record boasting of a literal 200 million man army?

Answer: _____

God also prophesied that the flesh of human beings would disintegrate to the bone while they are still in a standing position.

Zechariah 14:12, "This is the plague with which the Lord will strike all the nations that fought against Jerusalem: Their flesh will rot while they are still standing on their feet, their eyes will rot in their sockets, and their tongues will rot in their mouths."

This could be a "graphic description" of either " _____ _____ _____;" or perhaps "from a _____ weapon"?

- ✓ Since the year 2000, the U.S. and Russia combined have enough nuclear bombs to destroy planet earth _____ times over.
- ✓ Even smaller countries have their own supply of nuclear weapons right today.
- In these last days millions of people will have a hard time receiving what?

Answer: _____ _____

It will be just like it was in _____ day as Luke 17:28-30 tells us:

"People went about their daily business – eating and drinking, buying and selling, farming and building – until the morning Lot left Sodom. Then fire and burning sulfur rained down from heaven and destroyed them all. Yes, it will be "business as usual" right up to the hour when the Son of Man returns."

Jesus Himself declared, "When these things begin to take place, stand up and lift up your heads, because our redemption is drawing near." (Luke 21:28)

Will you stand up, and lift up your heads and hearts for Jesus in these last days before His Coming Again?

Chapter Four

The Rise of Falsehood

In the last chapter we talked about the importance of having a successful BBQ, remember? And there we saw that, try as we might, it's hard for us men to please our wives, right guys? And so for some of you ladies who might have been a little discouraged at our "manly" behavior, I want to encourage you. You see, it may not seem like it at times, but we men actually know a lot about you women. That's right! And to prove my point, I came across a list of the Top 10 Things Men Know About Women.[1] Get ready men, it's our time to shine!

1.
2.
3.
4.
5.
6.
7.
8.
9.
10.

Okay, so maybe us men are just a little clueless when it comes to understanding you women. But hey men, don't feel too bad, because we're not alone. A lot of people are not only clueless on marital issues, but Biblical ones as well. Especially when it comes to prophecy. And because of this, and the fact that they do not want to give their lives to Jesus, sadly they are running the risk of being left behind. And they will be catapulted into the seven-year Tribulation that is coming upon the whole world.

And folks, the time of the Tribulation is not a party. It's an outpouring of God's wrath upon a wicked and rebellious planet. In fact, Jesus said in **Matthew 24** that it would be a time of greater horror than anything the world has ever seen or will ever see again. He also said that unless that time of calamity is shortened, the entire human race would be destroyed. But God is not only a God of wrath; He's a God of love as well. And **because He loves you and I**, He has given us many warning signs so that we would know when the Tribulation could be near and that Christ's 2nd Coming is rapidly approaching.

Therefore, to keep us from being clueless about the dangers of being left behind, we're going to continue taking a look at **The Final Countdown**. We already saw how the **#10** sign on **The Final Countdown** was **The Jewish People**. The **#9** sign was **Modern Technology** and in the last chapter we saw how the **#8** sign was none other than **Worldwide Upheaval**. And there we saw that God lovingly foretold you and I that when we see an **Increase of Earthquakes, Famines, Pestilence**, and **Wars** that it would be an indicator that we are in the last days.

But that's not the only signs that God has given us. The **#7** sign on **The Final Countdown** is none other than **The Rise of Falsehood**. So just what are these specific prophesies being fulfilled today concerning **The Rise of**

Falsehood, revealing that we could be in the last days? Well, I'm glad you asked. Let's take a look. The **1ˢᵗ End Time Prophecy** concerning **The Rise of Falsehood** is that there would be an **Increase of False Christs**.

Luke 21:5-8 "Some of His disciples were remarking about how the temple was adorned with beautiful stones and with gifts dedicated to God. But Jesus said, As for what you see here, the time will come when not one stone will be left on another; every one of them will be thrown down. Teacher, they asked, when will these things happen? And what will be the sign that they are about to take place? He replied: Watch out that you are not deceived. For many will come in my name, claiming, 'I am he,' and, 'The time is near.' Do not follow them." (NIV)

According to our text there, one of the biggest and most obvious signs and **the very first thing out of Jesus' mouth** to indicate when we are in the last days is when there will be an **Increase of False Christs**. Now, throughout history we've had a few people here and there claiming to be Jesus. That's pretty commonplace. But what's **not common** is how, **in the last century alone**, there has been an explosion of people claiming to be the Messiah. For instance, one such person is the Reverend Sun Myung Moon of the moonies who has tons of followers. He not only claims to be the "messiah" and the "lord of the universe" but he has even stated that Jesus follows him.

"Jesus Christ is trying to follow me, my footsteps, all the way. He stayed in Paradise, because he did not marry. But I gave him marriage. Don't you want to meet the wives of Buddha, Confucius and Muhammad? They sent letters of gratitude to me from the spirit world. They pledge that even if their religion disappears, they will follow me."[2]

Oh, but that's not all. You could also check out the "Jesus of Siberia" who has thousands of his own disciples who think he is Jesus "reincarnated" (not resurrected) sent to save the earth. In his crimson robe and long brown hair, his devotees say that he radiates incredible love, and speaking to him is like an electric shock or like bells ringing. And in case you doubt, he has stated, "It's all very complicated. But to keep things simple, yes, I am Jesus Christ."[3]

But hey, for those of you who don't want to travel all the way to Russia, today in Pennsylvania you could visit "What's Your Name." And the reason people call him that is because when they ask him, "What's your name," he will only reply back, "What's Your name?" Sounds like an annoying version of the messiah to me, how about you? Yet he has thousands of people visiting him whom state, "I was in his presence for an hour and felt unbelievable."[4]

And for those of you who want a Messiah bigger then Pennsylvania can offer, you can check out Lord Maitreya of which thousands of people all over the world consider to be Jesus. His appearance is supposed to have spawned "healing springs," "weeping and bleeding statues," and even "divine messages inscribed by the seeds within fruit and vegetables."[5]

Now, as amazing as this all sounds, the point is that these guys are not the only ones claiming to be Christ. **Right now, here in the United States alone, there are an estimated 10,000 people claiming to be Jesus.**[6] And speaking of the United States, right now there's a man named Jose Luis de Miranda going around claiming to be the literal second coming of Jesus Christ, teaching that there is no such thing as sin or hell, and asks his followers to tattoo 666, which he says is a good symbol, on their bodies as a sign of their allegiance to him. Yet, what's even more amazing is that people not only do, but he has tens of thousands of followers all over the world doing it![7]

In fact, every year in Jerusalem, a strange phenomenon is occurring that has been dubbed the Jerusalem Syndrome, where tens of thousands of people have delusions of being a Biblical character or Jesus Christ Himself.[8] And the sad thing is that people don't know that they are actually **being prepared by these**

false christs to one day worship and follow the ultimate false christ, the antichrist, who will say he is a god during the Tribulation.

2 Thessalonians 2:3-4 "Don't let anyone deceive you in any way, for that day will not come until the rebellion occurs and the man of lawlessness is revealed, the man doomed to destruction. He will oppose and exalt himself over everything that is called God or is worshipped, so that he sets himself up in God's temple, proclaiming himself to be God." (NIV)

Can you see how people are being prepared **right now** for the worship of the antichrist? During the tribulation, people will actually think that worshipping a man is a good thing. Pretty slick isn't it? Now, I don't know about you guys, but **in the last century alone**, it sure sounds like there's been a huge **Increase of False Christs**. Just like the Bible said. When? In the last days.

The **2nd End Time Prophecy** concerning **The Rise of Falsehood** is that there will be and **Increase of False Teachers**.

2 Peter 2:1-2 "But there were also false prophets in Israel, just as there will be false teachers among you. They will cleverly teach their destructive heresies about God and even turn against their Master who bought them. Theirs will be a swift and terrible end. Many will follow their evil teaching and shameful immorality. And because of them, Christ and his true way will be slandered." (NLT)

According to our text there, another one of the biggest and most obvious signs to indicate when the last days would be approaching is when there would be an **Increase of False Teachers**. Now, throughout history we've had several groups of people who have brought forth false teachings that slander Christ's Name. That's been commonplace. But what's **not common** is how, **in the last century alone**, there has been an explosion of false teachers. Today, we have to contend with a multitude of false teachers and their organizations such as Mormonism, Jehovah's Witnesses, Christian Science, and even some Charismatic fringe groups. And can you guess when each one of these began to flourish? That's right, all in the last century. But there's one other group of false teachers that I want to talk about that has also taken off in the last century. And that is none other than the **New Age Movement**. Like many of the other false teachings, the New Age Movement has its roots in the occult and satanism. In fact, it is my opinion that the New Age Movement is the single false teaching that is **right now preparing the world for a One World Religion**. It's a mixture of all religions where nothing is wrong, except for Christianity. To show you what I mean, let's take a look at some of the typical New Age beliefs:

1. All is god: the earth, man, animals, and plants.
2. Man is destroying the earth along with the animals and plants and unless he changes his ways, "Mother Earth" will be forced to destroy humanity.
3. Christianity is the biggest culprit in destroying the earth by teaching that man had dominion over the earth when the earth is a living being.
4. There is no such thing as sin and no need to repent and be saved.
5. Jesus is but one of many great teachers such as Buddha, Muhammad or Confucius.
6. Mankind should seek direction directly from "the spirit world" via a psychic, a channeler, a palm reader, astrology, angels, space aliens, dead relatives, meditation, etc.
7. All religions (except orthodox Christianity) are of equal merit.
8. In order for the world to be at peace and harmony there must be "New World Order, Universal monetary system, World authority on food, health, and water, Universal tax, and military draft, One world leader, and the abolishment of Christianity.[9]

Now, as you guys can see, those are some serious false teachings. In fact, you might be tempted to think that nobody in their right mind would ever fall for such heresy. Yet, as of 1995, New Agers represented twenty percent of the population in the United States, making them the third largest religious group.[10] So the question is, "How are they able to get so many converts in America?" Well, as is the case with many of the false teachers, the New Age Movement has gone underground and is winning converts right under our noses.

And the **1st way** the New Age Movement is seducing people is by promoting a **Healthy Earth**. That's right, I'm talking about the **Environmental Movement**. Little do people know that the teachings of environmentalism have roots in the occultic beliefs of the New Age Movement. The average person thinks that they are helping to **save the earth**, when in reality they are helping to spread the beliefs of the New Age Movement. Stop and think for a moment what the Environmental Movement teaches. Do they not believe that the earth, plants and animals are sacred, almost to the point of worship? Do they not say that man and Christianity are the biggest culprits in the destruction of the earth? Do they not promote a return to more "earth-centered" religions, and a global movement to unify people to save the earth? In fact, one of the biggest environmental groups, the Sierra Club, has gone on record as stating this:

"'Turn to the traditions of ancient cultures' such as Buddhist meditations and Native American Hopi rituals in order to 'reaffirm our bond with the spirit of the living earth. The more you contact the voice of the living earth and evaluate what it says, the easier it will become for you to contact it and trust what it provides.'"[11]

Now, that sure sounds like New Age teachings to me, how about you? You see, there's nothing wrong with having a healthy earth. The problem is when you place the earth before man, and begin to worship it above God. Besides, people don't know that they are actually being prepared via the environmental movement **to explain away the earth's catastrophes** that will take place during the Tribulation.

Revelation 8:7,9,11 "Hail and fire mixed with blood were thrown down upon the earth, and one-third of the earth was set on fire. One-third of the trees were burned, and all the grass was burned. And one-third of all things living in the sea died. One-third of the water bitter, and many people died because the water was so bitter." (NLT)

Now, we all know that this is speaking of the judgment from God Almighty during the time of the Tribulation. But your average environmentalist is being taught this:

"Climatic shifts, droughts, floods, acid rain and pollution, earthquakes, and volcanic eruptions. Although severe, these changes will pave the way for a cleansing of the earth and a new relationship between earth and man.

This will be the Day of Purification. Trees will die. Cold places will become hot. Hot places will become cold. Lands will sink into the ocean and lands will rise out of the sea.

All the suffering going on in this country with the tornadoes, floods, and earthquakes is carried on the breath of Mother Earth because she is in pain. This battle will cleanse the heart of people and restore our Mother Earth from illness, and the wicked will be gotten rid of."[12]

Can you see how people are being prepared **right now** for the earth catastrophes that will come one day? People during the Tribulation will actually think that the catastrophes from God are a good thing. Pretty slick isn't it? And it's all because they are being seduced by the New Age Movement promoting a Healthy Earth.

The **2nd way** the New Age Movement is seducing people is by promoting a **Healthy Body**. That's right, I'm talking about the **Vegetarian Movement**. Little do people know that the tenets of vegetarianism have roots in the occultic beliefs of the New Age Movement. The average person thinks that they are helping to **save the animals**, when in reality they are helping to spread the beliefs of the New Age Movement. Stop and think for a moment what the Vegetarian Movement teaches. Do they not believe that the earth, plants and **especially animals** are sacred, almost to the point of worship? One such group is SERV. The Society of Ethical Religious Vegetarians.[13] Do they not say that man and Christianity are the biggest culprits in the destruction of the earth via the eating of animals? Do they not promote a global movement to unify people to save the animals? Now that sure sounds like New Age teachings to me, how about you? You see, there's nothing wrong with having a healthy body. The problem is when you place animals before man, and begin to worship them above God. Besides, people don't know that they are being prepared via the vegetarian movement **to explain away a false teaching on the restriction of certain foods** that the Apostle Paul said would appear on the scene in the last days.

1 Timothy 4:2-3 "These teachers are hypocrites and liars. They pretend to be religious, but their consciences are dead. They will say it is wrong to be married and wrong to eat certain foods. But God created those foods to be eaten with thanksgiving by people who know and believe the truth." (NLT)

Now, we all know that its okay to eat any kind of food, especially meat, **since God said to** after the flood in Genesis Chapter 9. But your average vegetarian is being taught this:

"We need an interfaith effort to gain a more humane, just, peaceful, and environmentally sustainable world. We believe that by applying spiritual values to scientific knowledge encourages plant-based diets, with major benefits to humans, animals, and the environment.

It is essential that there is a major shift toward vegetarianism to end diseases, horrible mistreatment of animals, threats to ecosystems, global climate change, wasteful use of water, land, fuel, widespread hunger, and increasing violence.

Through the efforts of environmentalists, vegetarians, and animal rights activists, the earth will become a healthier, happier place for all species to live."[14]

Can you see how people are being prepared **right now** for a false teaching that Paul said would come in the last days? People will actually think that a "controlled diet" is a good thing. Pretty slick isn't it? And it's all because they are being seduced by the New Age Movement promoting a Healthy Body.

The **3rd way** the New Age Movement is seducing people is by promoting a **Heavenly Host**. That's right, I'm talking about the **Angels Craze and the UFO Movement**. Little do people know that the tenets of the messages supposedly coming from angels and UFOs have their roots in the occultic beliefs of the New Age Movement. The average person thinks that they are **making contact and receiving new teachings** from these heavenly hosts, when in reality they are helping to spread the beliefs of the New Age Movement via **demonic deception**. To show you what I mean, let's take a look at the teachings that are coming from these supposed angels and UFO's:

1. All of us are little gods.
2. The earth is a living entity and we need to worship her and change our ways or we will be destroyed.
3. Jesus, Muhammad, and Buddha all came from the ET's to assist mankind in our next step of evolution.
4. There is no such thing as sin; we do not need to be saved.
5. Orthodox Christianity has it all wrong. Jesus' real message was to teach us that each one of us could become "christs."
6. To aid in contacting these "heavenly beings" one should refrain from certain foods and practice meditation
7. Mankind needs to unite into a one-world government and religion or we will be destroyed.
8. The devil or Lucifer is actually a good guy who has come to free us.[15]

Now, that sure sounds like New Age teachings to me, how about you? Besides, why would these beings come all the way to earth just to promote occultic New Age teachings and practices and debunk Christianity? That's sounds demonic! And why is it that UFO experts are saying that these beings are not so much physical in nature but **spiritual** because they clock them at speeds up to 16,000 miles an hour making right turns which would instantly destroy anything that is physical. Hmmm. Demons are spiritual, aren't they? And why is it that the top UFO experts are now saying that based on decades of research, these beings aren't coming from outer space but **inner space**. They're coming from another dimension. Hmmm. Demons come from another dimension called the spirit realm. And why is it that there's only one way on record to get rid of these beings when they do come your way. And that's when you **command them in the Name of Jesus Christ to leave** and they do?[16] Gee whiz folks, maybe it's just me, but that sure sounds like a demon. Therefore, if it walks like a demon, and talks like a demon, and acts like a demon, I'd kind of say, we're dealing with demons here!

And then as if that wasn't enough proof that we're dealing with actual demonic entities here, little do people know that they are being prepared via the Angels and UFO teachings **to explain away the rapture of the Church**, which takes place prior to the time of the Tribulation.

1 Thessalonians 4:15-17 "I can tell you this directly from the Lord. We who are still living when the Lord returns will not rise to meet him ahead of those who are in their graves. For the Lord himself will come down from heaven with a commanding shout, with the call of the archangel, and with the trumpet call of God. First, all the Christians who have died will rise from their graves. Then, together with them, we who are still alive and remain on the earth will be caught up in the clouds to meet the Lord in the air and remain with him forever." (NLT)

Now, we all know that this is clearly referring to the evacuation of the Christians from the earth right before God's wrath is poured out upon the world. But your average Angel and UFO enthusiasts are being taught this:

"There will be great shiftings within humanity on this planet. It will seem that great chaos and turmoil are forming, that nations are rising against each other in war, and that earthquakes are happening more frequently. Earth is shaking itself free, and a certain realignment or adjustment period is to be expected.

The people who leave the planet during the time of earth changes do not fit here any longer, and they are stopping the harmony of earth. When the time comes that perhaps twenty million people leave the planet at one time, there will be a tremendous shift in consciousness for those who are remaining."[17]

People of God, you talk about the ultimate excuse. Imagine the day when thousands of people worldwide are going to disappear from the planet via the rapture. The whole world will be in a state of absolute panic and wondering, hoping, groping for some answer **and then** somebody gets up and says, "Don't worry. Your loved ones are just fine. They've been beamed up by UFO's and are awaiting the time of rehabilitation when they can join us back here on earth safely as we now enter the Age of Uptopia." People of God, wake up! We are living in the last days! We are seeing for the first time in mankind's history how people are being prepared **right now to explain away** the rapture of the Church, even to the point where people will actually think that being left behind is a good thing. Tell me that's not demonic! And it's all because they are being seduced by the New Age Movement promoting a Heavenly Host. Pretty slick, isn't it?

You see, there's nothing wrong with Heavenly Hosts. There are holy angels from God. Yet there are also deceptive demons working for satan. And the problem is when you place demonic teachings before God's Word and begin to follow them instead of the Bible; which is exactly what God said would happen in the last days.

1 Timothy 4:1 "Now the Holy Spirit tells us clearly that in the last times some will turn away from what we believe; they will follow lying spirits and teachings that come from demons." (NLT)

Now, I don't know about you guys, but it sure sounds like, **in the last century alone**, there has been a huge **Increase of False Teachers**. Just like the Bible said. When? In the last days.

And believe it or not, even with all this amazing evidence pointing to the signs of Christ's soon return, some people still refuse to listen to any kind of request, like this lady:

"In the 18th-century in England, a vagabond was exhausted and famished, when he came to a roadside inn with a sign reading, 'George and the Dragon.' So the hungry man knocked on the door of the inn.

At this, the innkeeper's wife stuck her head out a window, so the vagabond asked, 'Could ye spare some porridge?'

The woman took one look at his shabby, dirty clothes and shouted, 'No!'

Then the man asked, 'Well then, could I have a pint of broth?'

And without missing a beat the woman yelled back, 'No!'

Undaunted, the vagabond now requested, 'Could I at least use your washroom?'

But the woman just shouted back again, 'No!'

Well at this the vagabond said, 'Might I please...?'

'What now?' the woman screeched, not allowing him to finish.

'D'ye suppose,' he asked, 'that I might have a word with George?'"[18]

Now, that lady didn't want to listen to any requests did she? But believe it or not, she's not alone. The Bible said that in the last days, many people would refuse to listen to God's request to repent and be saved before it's too late.

Revelation 3:3 "Remember, therefore, what you have received and heard; obey it, and repent. But if you do not wake up, I will come like a thief, and you will not know at what time I will come to you." (NIV)

People of God, I hope you're not one of those who are refusing to listen to God's loving request to be saved. Why? Because if you are, you might wake up one day and discover that **you've been left behind**. And you know what? God doesn't want you left behind. Because He loves you and I, He has given us the warning sign of **The Rise of Falsehood** to show us that the Tribulation could be near and that Christ's 2nd Coming is rapidly approaching. Jesus Himself said this:

Luke 21:28 "When these things begin to take place, stand up and lift up your heads, because your redemption is drawing near." (NIV)

Like it or not folks, we are headed for **The Final Countdown**. We don't know the day or the hour. Only God knows. The point is, if you're a Christian, you need to know that all we are given in this life is a little bitty dash between two dates. I am of course speaking in regards to the dash on our tombstones. Therefore, life is short, pray hard and take somebody to heaven with you, will you? Folks, it's high time we Christians speak up and declare the good news of salvation to those who are dying all around us. But please, if you're not a Christian, give your life to Jesus today, because tomorrow may be too late! Just like the Bible said!

Study Questions

Review

Jesus Christ is coming very, very soon! So far, Pastor Billy has shared three explosive and prophetic signs that prove that the above statement is true.

Can you recall what they were?

Sign #10 is _____ _____ _____

Sign #9 is _____ _____

Sign #8 is _____ _____

Under this last sign, there were four indicators that we are in the last days. We would see an "increase of _____, _____,

_____, and _____."

This Chapter:

The #7 sign on The Final Countdown is none other than _____

_____ _____ _____

THE 1ST END TIME PROPHECY CONCERNING THE RISE OF

FALSEHOOD IS THAT THERE WOULD BE AN INCREASE OF

_____ _____ .

Jesus warned in Luke 21:8"Watch out that you are not deceived. For many will come in my name, claiming, "I am he", and "the time is near". "Do not follow them."

The first such person Pastor Billy mentions is the Reverend _____

_____ _____ of the Moonies, or the

"Unification Church". Moon claims to be _____;

_____ of the _____ and that "Jesus Christ is

trying to _____ _____, my footsteps, all the way."

But that's not all

A second false christ is _____ of _____ .

- What do his followers think he is?

Answer: Jesus " _____ " sent to save the earth.

- What did this man boldly claim?

Answer: "To keep things simple, yes, I am Jesus Christ."

But it's not over yet,

There's a man in Pennsylvania called, _____

_____ _____. This is how he actually responds to a

person who would ask him, "what's your name?" He replies, "What's Your

Name". But it doesn't matter what his name sounds like. People continue to be

captivated by his presence. Thousands who visit him declare, "I was in his

presence for an hour and felt unbelievable."

But still another false christ that thousands around the world consider to be the

Messiah is _____ _____. To some, he is so powerful

that his appearance is supposed to have spawned _____

_____, _____, and _____ statues, and

even _____ messages inscribed by the seeds within

_____ and _____."

- Right now in the United States alone, what is the estimated number of
   those claiming to be Jesus?

Answer: _____

There's another man in the U.S. named _____

_____ _____ _____ who claims to

be the literal second coming of Jesus Christ.

Note a few of his teachings: "There is no such thing as _____ or

_____, the 666 tattoo his followers wear is a

_____ _____.

But there's still more

- What happens every year in Jerusalem that has been dubbed "The

   Jerusalem Syndrome?"

Answer: Tens of thousands of people have _____ of being a

Biblical character or _____ _____ Himself.

Pastor Billy mentioned, "the sad thing is that people don't know that they are

actually being prepared by these false christs to one day worship and follow the

ultimate false christ, the _____.."

2 Thessalonians 2:3-4;

Don't let anyone _____ you in any way, for that day will not come

until the rebellion occurs and the man of _____ is revealed,

the man _____ to _____. He will oppose and

exalt himself over everything that is called God or is worshiped, so that be sets

himself up in God's temple, proclaiming himself to be _____.

> # THE 2ND END TIME PROPHECY CONCERNING THE RISE OF FALSEHOOD IS THAT THERE WILL BE AN INCREASE OF
>
> _____ _____.

2 Peter 2:1-2; "But there were also false prophets in Israel, just as there will be _____ _____among you. They will cleverly teach their _____ heresies about God and even turn against their Master who bought them. Theirs will be a swift and terrible end. Many will follow their _____ _____ and shameful immorality. And because of them, Christ and his true way will be slandered."

There's a multitude of false teachers that the Church has to contend with today.

Some of their organizations are: _____, Jehovah's

Witnesses, _____ _____, and even some

_____ fringe groups." One other group of false teachers that

we must highlight is the _____ _____

_____.

- From where does the New Age Movement have its roots?

Answer: The _____ and _____."

- What is the New Age Movement preparing the world for right now?

Answer: A "_____ _____ _____."

What are some of the typical New Age beliefs:

1. All is god: the earth, man, animals, and plants.

2. Man is destroying the earth along with the animals and plants and unless he changes his ways, "Mother Earth" will be forced to destroy humanity.

3. Christianity is the biggest culprit in destroying the earth by teaching that man had dominion over the earth when the earth is a living being.

4. There is no such thing as sin and no need to repent and be saved.

5. Jesus is but one of many great teachers such as Buddha, Muhammad or Confucius.

6. Mankind should seek direction directly from "the spirit world" via a psychic, a channeler, a palm reader, astrology, angels, space aliens, dead relatives, meditation, etc.

7. All religions (except orthodox Christianity) are of equal merit.

8. In order for the world to be at peace and harmony there must be "New World Order, universal monetary system, world authority on food, health, and water, universal tax, and military draft, one world leader, and the abolishment of Christianity.

As of 1995, New Agers represented twenty percent of the population in the United States, making them the third largest religious group. How are they making so many converts in America?

The 1ˢᵗ Way the New Age Movement is seducing people is by promoting

_____ _____ _____.

The teachings of environmentalism have roots in the occultic beliefs of the New Age Movement. Those who think they are saving the earth are in reality "helping to spread the beliefs of the **New Age Movement**.

- What does the Environmental Movement teach?

Answer: The earth, plants and animals are _____ man and Christianity are the biggest culprits in the _____ of the earth they "promote a return to more _____ _____ religions, and a _____ movement to unify people to _____ the earth.

Pastor Billy agrees that there's nothing wrong with having a healthy earth; but he parts company with those who place the earth _____ man, and begin to _____ it above _____.

- And how will these environmentalists explain away the earth's

    catastrophes that will take place during the Tribulation? for example,

Revelation 8:7, 9, 11, Hail and fire mixed with blood were thrown down upon the earth, and one-third of the earth was set on fire. One-third of the trees were burned, and all the grass was burned. And one-third of all things living in the sea died. One third of the water bitter, and many people died because the water was so bitter.

These changes will pave the way for a _____ of the earth and

a new _____ between earth and man.

This will be the Day of _____. All the suffering going on

in this country with the tornadoes, floods, and earthquakes is carried on the

breath of Mother Earth because she is in pain. This battle will

_____ the heart of people and _____ our Mother

Earth from _____, and the _____ will be gotten rid

of." People during the time of God's wrath on this earth will actually think

"that the catastrophes from God are a _____

thing.

The 2ⁿᵈ Way the New Age Movement is seducing people is by promoting

a _____ _____.

The tenets of vegetarianism have roots in the _____ beliefs of

the New Age Movement. People who think they are saving the animals are,

in reality, helping to spread the beliefs of the New Agers.

The Society of Ethical Religious Vegetarians (SERV) says that via the

_____ of _____, man and Christianity

are the biggest culprits in the destruction of the earth. They promote a global

move to "_____ people to _____ the

_____."

- What does the Vegetarian Movement teach?

Answer: The earth, plants and *especially animals* are sacred.

Nothing wrong with having a healthy body, but the problem surfaces "when

you place animals _____ man, and begin to

_____ them above _____."

Via the vegetarian movement, people are being prepared to explain away a false

teaching on the _____ of certain foods that the Apostle Paul

said would appear on the scene in the last days.

I Timothy 4:2-3 states, "These teachers are hypocrites and liars. They pretend to
be religious, but their consciences are dead. They will say it is wrong to eat
certain foods. But God created those foods to be eaten with thanksgiving by
people who know and believe the truth.

- What is your average vegetarian being taught?

Answer: "We believe that by applying spiritual values to scientific knowledge

encourages _____ _____ diets, with major benefits

to humans, animals, and the environment."

"It is essential that there is a major shift toward _____ to end

_____ , horrible mistreatment of animals, threats to

ecosystems, global climate change, wasteful use of water, land, fuel, widespread

hunger, and increasing violence."

"Through the efforts of _____, _____, and

_____ _____ activists, the earth will become a

_____, _____ place for all species to

live."

The 3rd Way the New Age Movement is seducing people is by promoting a

_____ _____.

One could also call it the _____Craze and the

_____Movement.

People don't know that the tenets of the messages supposedly coming from

angels and UFOs have their roots in the occultic beliefs of the New Age

Movement.

- By making contact and receiving the new teachings from these heavenly

    hosts, what are people actually doing?

Answer: They are helping to spread the beliefs of the New Age Movement via

_____ – _____.

Note the teachings that are coming from these supposed angels and UFO's:

1.   All of us are little gods.

2.   The earth is a living entity and we need to worship her and change our ways or we will be destroyed.

3.   Jesus, Muhammad, and Buddha all came from the ET's to assist mankind in our next step of evolution.

4.   There is no such thing as sin; we do not need to be saved.

5.   Orthodox Christianity has it all wrong. Jesus' real message was to teach us that each one of us could become "christs."

6.   To aid in contacting these "heavenly beings" one should refrain from certain foods and practice meditation.

7.   Mankind needs to unite into a one-world government and religion or we will be destroyed.

8.   The devil or Lucifer is actually a good guy who has come to free us.

Pastor Billy shares some reasons why these entities connected with UFO's are really demons.

1. They _____ occultic New Age teachings and practices.

2. They _____ Christianity.

3. UFO experts are admitting that these beings aren't so much physical in nature but _____.

4. They have been clocked at speeds of up to _____, and making right turns at that speed, which would destroy anything that is physical.

5. UFO experts are also saying that, after extensive research, these beings "aren't coming from outer space but _____

_____…from another _____,";

which we believe is the _____ realm.

There's only one way on record to get rid of these beings, when they do come your way: _____ them in the _____ of Jesus Christ to leave.

People also do not know that they are being prepared via the Angels and UFO teachings to explain away the _____ of the Church.

1 Thessalonians 4:15-17 "I can tell you this directly from the Lord. We who are still living when the Lord returns will not rise to meet him ahead of those who are in their graves. For the Lord himself will come down from heaven with a commanding shout, with the call of the archangel, and with the trumpet call of God. First, all the Christians who have died will rise from their graves. Then, together with them, we who are still alive and remain on the earth will be caught up in the clouds to meet the Lord in the air and remain with him forever."

We all know that this refers to the evacuation of the Christians from the earth before God's wrath is poured out upon the ungodly.

But what is your average Angel and UFO enthusiast being taught?

"There will be great shifting within humanity on this planet. It will seem that great chaos and turmoil are forming, that nations are rising against each other in war, and that earthquakes are happening more frequently. Earth is shaking itself free, and a certain realignment or adjustment period is to be expected.

The people who leave the planet during the time of earth changes do not fit here any longer, and they are stopping the harmony of earth. When the time comes that perhaps twenty million people leave the planet at one time, there will be a tremendous shift in consciousness for those who are remaining."

Warning: Beloved, there are deceptive demons working for satan who are gathering followers through demonic teachings; just like the Bible said would happen in the last days.

1 Timothy 4:1 warns,

Now the Holy Spirit tells us clearly that in the last times some will turn away

from what we believe; they will follow _____ spirits and

teachings that come from _____.

The Rise of Falsehood clearly indicates that Christ's 2nd coming is rapidly

approaching. And what is Jesus' admonition to his people?

Luke 21:28, "When these things begin to take place, stand up and lift up your heads, because your redemption is drawing near."

Jesus is coming again! Is your heart ready to meet Him?

Chapter Five

The Rise of Wickedness

"An old preacher was dying and had very little time left on earth. So he sent a message for an IRS agent and a local politician, both church members, to come to his home. When they arrived, they were ushered up to his bedroom. As they entered the room, the preacher held out his hands and motioned for them to sit on each side of the bed. Then the dying preacher grasped their hands, sighed contentedly, smiled and stared at the ceiling.

For a time, no one said anything. Both the IRS agent and politician were touched and flattered that the old preacher would ask them to be with him during his final moment. But they were also puzzled at why he wanted them there. Plus they both remembered his many long, uncomfortable sermons about greed, covetousness and their wicked behavior that made them squirm in their seats. And finally they couldn't take it anymore so the politician asked, 'Preacher, why did you ask the two of us to come?'

And the old preacher mustered up his last bit of strength and then said weakly, 'Well, Jesus died between two thieves, and that's how I want to go, too.'"[1]

Now, that preacher wanted to make sure that he had made adequate preparations before leaving this earth, didn't he? That's very important. But unfortunately, most people don't have this attitude. You see, the average person refrains from thinking about what's going to happen to them when they die. And to make matters worse, they keep putting off getting right with God through Jesus Christ. And because of this, they are sadly running the risk of being left behind. They will be catapulted into the seven-year Tribulation that is coming upon the whole world.

And folks, the time of the Tribulation is not a party. It's an outpouring of God's wrath upon a wicked and rebellious planet. In fact, Jesus said in **Matthew 24** that it would be a time of greater horror than anything the world has ever seen or will ever see again. He also said that unless that time of calamity is shortened, the entire human race would be destroyed. But God is not only a God of wrath; He's a God of love as well. And **because He loves you and I**, He has given us many warning signs so that we would know when the Tribulation could be near and that Christ's 2nd Coming is rapidly approaching. Therefore, to help us make adequate preparations so we won't be left behind, we're going to continue taking a look at **The Final Countdown**.

We already saw how the **#10** sign on **The Final Countdown** was **The Jewish People**. The **#9** sign was **Modern Technology**. The **#8** sign was **Worldwide Upheaval** and in the last chapter we saw how the **#7** sign was none other than **The Rise of Falsehood**. There we saw that God lovingly foretold you and I that when we see an **Increase of False Christs** and an **Increase of False Teachers**, that this would be an indicator that we are in the last days.

But that's not the only signs that God has given us. The **#6** sign on **The Final Countdown** is none other than **The Rise of Wickedness**. So just what are these specific prophesies being fulfilled today concerning **The Rise of Wickedness**, revealing that we could be in the last days? Well, I'm glad you asked. Let's take a look. The **1st End Time Prophecy** concerning **The Rise of Wickedness** is that people would love themselves more than God.

2 Timothy 3:1-5 "But mark this: There will be terrible times in the last days. People will be lovers of themselves, lovers of money, boastful, proud, abusive, disobedient to their parents, ungrateful, unholy, without love, unforgiving, slanderous, without self-control, brutal, not lovers of the good, treacherous, rash, conceited, lovers of pleasure rather than lovers of God— having a form of godliness but denying its power. Have nothing to do with them." (NIV)

According to this passage of Scripture, one of the major characteristics of society in the last days is one that would be filled with unadulterated wickedness. And the root of this wicked behavior stems from a **love of self instead of a love for God**. Now, throughout history we've always had some form of wicked behavior. That's been commonplace. But what's **not common** is how **in the last century alone**, there has been an explosion of **every single one** of these wicked behaviors that Paul listed here. And it's only getting worse. In fact, in all honesty, **we're no longer shocked** at this kind of wickedness because it's now considered the norm. And lest we forget how rotten things are, we're reminded daily of it on every single news station, twenty-four hours a day. And keep in mind that not long ago the top discipline problems in schools **used to be** talking, chewing gum, making noise, running in halls, getting out of turn in line, and not putting paper in the wastebasket.[2] And to show you the fruits of a society that loves itself more than God and how fast this produces wickedness, let's take a look at the change of behavior in America in **just the last 30 years**.

1. Violent Crimes are up 995%.
2. The inmate population has grown from about 200,000 to nearly 2 ½ million or about one out of every 99 adults. America now has more people per capita in prison than any nation on earth.
3. Unmarried couples living together are up 725%.
4. Illegitimate births are up 400%.
5. The divorce rate is now 60%.
6. In some parts of California the rate of divorce is one for every marriage.
7. A murder occurs every 23 minutes.
8. A rape occurs every 6 minutes.

9. An aggravated assault occurs every 48 seconds.
10. An abortion takes place every 20 seconds.
11. A burglary occurs every 8 seconds.
12. Sexually transmitted diseases among 10-14 yr. olds are up 385%.
13. Unwed pregnancies among 10-14 yr. olds are up 553%.
14. Teenage suicide is up 200%.
15. The national average of SAT scores has dropped 80 points.
16. Across America, 25% of graduating seniors couldn't read their diploma.
17. Every day 13 youth commit suicide, 16 are murdered, 1,000 become mothers, 100,000 bring guns to school, 2,200 drop put of school, 500 begin using drugs, 1,000 begin drinking alcohol, 3,500 are assaulted, 630 are robbed, and 80 are raped.
18. More people have died in America in the last 30 years from murders and suicides then from all the wars in the history of the United States.[3]

Now I don't know about you guys, but **in the last 30 years alone**, it sure sounds like there's been a massive **Rise of Wickedness**, hasn't there? Just like the Bible said. When? In the last days.

But the question is, "How could there be such an explosion of wickedness in such a short amount of time, especially in America with our Godly heritage? How could a Christian nation turn from loving God to loving themselves?" Great question, I'm glad you asked. And the **1st reason** why people have turned from loving God to loving themselves, causing this **Rise of Wickedness**, is because of the promotion of a **Wicked Worldview**. That's right, I'm talking about **humanism**. Little do people know that the teachings of humanism have actually aided in this **massive rise of wicked behavior**. For those of you who may not know, humanism is the worldview where **man is the center of all things, not God**. And as you can tell, it is diametrically opposed to Christianity. But don't just take my word for it. Let's look at a few of there own statements of belief from the Humanist Manifesto I and II:

1. Faith in the prayer-hearing God, assumed to live and care for persons, to hear and understand their prayers, and to be able to do something about them, is an unproved and outmoded faith.
2. We find insufficient evidence for the belief in the existence of a supernatural. We begin with humans not God.
3. We do not accept as true the literal interpretation of the Old and New Testaments.
4. We include a recognition of an individual's right to die with dignity, euthanasia, suicide, birth control and abortion.
5. We believe that intolerant attitudes, often cultivated by orthodox religions and puritanical cultures, unduly repress sexual conduct. Divorce should be recognized. The many varieties of sexual exploration should not themselves be considered evil.
6. We oppose any tyranny over the mind of man to shackle free thought. In the past such tyrannies have been directed by churches and states attempting to enforce the edicts of religious bigots.
7. Promises of immortal salvation or fear of eternal damnation are both illusory and harmful.
8. Salvationism, based on mere affirmation, still appears as harmful, diverting people with false hopes of heaven hereafter. No deity will save us; we must save ourselves.[4]

Now, does this attitude sound familiar today? Of course it does. You see, it was humanists that forced the Bible, prayer, and the Ten Commandments out of the schools under the premise that religion and education do not mix. Yet, what most people don't realize is that **the Supreme Court considered humanism a religion** back in the early 1960's. And can you guess just whose "religious" teachings are filling the schools without even being questioned? That's right, humanism! I believe that's called having your cake and eating it too! And today, faithful and godly teachers not only have to contend with wicked behavior in the classroom, but also with the wicked goals of humanists who have a **different agenda** for teaching children. Listen to their own words:

• "(Our) great object was to get rid of Christianity, and to convert our churches into halls of science. The plan was not to make open attacks on religion...but to establish a system of state schools, from which all religion was to be excluded...and to which all parents were to be compelled by law to send their children. For this purpose, a secret society was formed and the whole country was to be organized." **Orestes Brownson (1803-1876)**

- "What the church has been for medieval man, the public school must become for democratic and rational man. God would be replaced by the concept of the public good." **Horace Mann (1796-1858)**

- "There is no God and there is no soul. Hence, there is no need for the props of traditional religion. With dogma and creed excluded, then immutable truth is also dead and buried. There is no room for fixed, natural law or moral absolutes." **John Dewey (1859-1952), the "Father of Progressive Education;" co-author of the first Humanist Manifesto and honorary NEA president**

- "Education is thus a most powerful ally of humanism, and every American school is a school of humanism. What can a theistic Sunday School's meeting for an hour once a week and teaching only a fraction of the children do to stem the tide of the five-day program of humanistic teaching?" **Charles F. Potter, Humanism: A New Religion (1930)**

- "I think that the most important factor moving us toward a secular society has been the educational factor. Our schools may not teach Johnny to read properly, but the fact that Johnny is in school until he is sixteen tends to lead toward the elimination of religious superstition." **Paul Blanshard, "Three Cheers for Our Secular State," The Humanist, March/April 1976**

- "We must ask how we can kill the God of Christianity. We need only to insure that our schools teach only secular knowledge. If we could achieve this, God would indeed be shortly due for a funeral service." **G. Richard Bozarth, "On Keeping God Alive," American Atheist, November 1977**

- "I am convinced that the battle for humankind's future must be waged and won in the public school classroom by teachers who correctly perceive their role as proselytizers of a new faith: a religion of humanity. These teachers must embody the same selfless dedication as the most rabid fundamentalist preachers, for they will be ministers of another sort, utilizing a classroom instead of a pulpit to convey humanist values in whatever subject they teach, regardless of educational level – preschool, day care or a large state university. The classroom must and will become an arena of conflict between the old and the new – the rotting corpse of Christianity...and the new faith of humanism." **John J. Dunphy, "A New Religion for a New Age," The Humanist, January/February 1983**

- "Every child in America entering school at the age of five is mentally ill, because he comes to school with certain allegiances toward our founding fathers, toward our elected officials, toward his parents, toward a belief in a supernatural Being, toward the sovereignty of this nation as a separate entity. It is up to you teachers to make all these sick children well by creating the international children of the future." **Harvard Professor of Education and Psychiatry, 1984** [5]

You see, the average person thinks that the teachings of humanism and the **triumph of the human spirit** is the antidote needed to cure the wickedness of the world. Yet, in reality they are actually following the teachings of the king of wickedness, satan.

Genesis 3:4-5 "'You won't die!' the serpent hissed. 'God knows that your eyes will be opened when you eat it. You will become just like God, knowing everything, both good and evil.'" (NLT)

Hmmm. You mean the teaching of man, being the center of all things, determining his own destiny, in fact, being his own god, started with satan? So is it any wonder that there has been such a massive **Rise of Wickedness** just like the Bible said? When? In the last days.

The **2nd reason** why people have turned from loving God to loving themselves, causing this **Rise of Wickedness**, is because of the promotion of a **Wicked Worship**. That's right, I'm talking about the **self-love**, **self-esteem movement**. Little do people know that the teachings of the self-love, self-esteem movement have actually aided in the **massive rise of wicked behavior**. And for those of you who may not know it, the self-love, self-esteem movement has its roots in the beliefs of such men as Sigmund Freud, who frequently used cocaine,[6] and Carl Jung, who not only had conversations with a box, but even had visions of God supposedly parting the clouds and relieving Himself on a Church building.[7] And these are the "founding fathers" of modern secular psychology? But there are two other psychologists who built on the ideas of Freud and Jung. Those men are Abraham Maslow and Carl Rogers.[8] They are the ones who are primarily responsible for this **explosion of self-worship**. They have convinced us that not only are we to love ourselves, but we **must do so at all costs**, even if it means ignoring sinful behavior, refraining from discipline, blaming others, and avoiding personal responsibility. Why? Well, they say if we force people to deal with their own wicked behavior then they will damage their self-esteem, which will ruin all hopes of having a fulfilling life.

You might think that nobody in their right mind would fall for this nonsense. Or would they? You see, it's **because of this self-worship** that parents in Connecticut have taken their son's school to court. Why? Because he was caught destroying school property and was expelled by the school. But the parents say that their son now has **"feelings of unworthiness"** and his **"self-worth"** has been damaged, so they're suing. Oh, but that's not all; in Maine, signs saying "Happy Holidays" and the singing of Christmas carols are being now being banned **for fear of making somebody feel excluded**. In fact, in Manhattan, **Mother's Day** is now being eliminated because some kids may not have a mother and this **could damage their self-esteem**. But apparently so do kickball and dodgeball and similar games. Why? Because they promote competitiveness and make some kids feel excluded and that's no longer tolerated.[9]

And folks, what's even crazier than this is that some people have actually **twisted the Scripture** to try to make the Bible say that we should love ourselves. Here's one of their favorite passages to try to do this:

Matthew 22:37-39 "Jesus replied, 'You must love the Lord your God with all your heart, all your soul, and all your mind.' This is the first and greatest commandment. A second is equally important: Love your neighbor as yourself.'" (NLT)

Well, there it is plain as day, love yourself right? Wrong! Notice there are **two commandments** given by Jesus, **not three**. One, to love God and two to love your neighbor. Yet some add in a third commandment to love yourself and say that unless you love yourself first, you won't have the ability to love God or your neighbor. Now that's some **serious twisting of the Scripture**, don't you think? Besides, keep in mind that it was **loving self more than God** that caused the **fall of man**! But I guess we should call that a "good thing" now. Yeah, right.

Oh, but the self-love, self-esteem proponents not only twist Scripture, they also **turn a blind eye** to obvious passages in the Bible that teach **not to love yourself**, and instead deal honestly with our sin:

Ezekiel 20:43 "There you will remember your conduct and all the actions by which you have defiled yourselves, and you will loathe yourselves for all the evil you have done." (NIV)

Romans 7:18, 24 "I know that nothing good lives in me, that is, in my sinful nature. What a wretched man I am! Who will rescue me from this body of death?" (NIV)

Ezekiel 36:31-32 "Then you will remember your evil ways and wicked deeds, and you will loathe yourselves for your sins and detestable practices. Be ashamed and disgraced for your conduct, O House of Israel!" (NIV)

Job 42:6 "Therefore I despise myself and repent in dust and ashes." (NIV)

2 Corinthians 5:15 "And he died for all, that those who live should no longer live for themselves but for him who died for them and was raised again." (NIV)

Luke 6:32-33,35 "If you love those who love you, what credit is that to you? Even 'sinners' love those who love them. And if you do good to those who are good to you, what credit is that to you? Even 'sinners' do that. But love your enemies, do good to them, and lend to them without expecting to get anything back." (NIV)

1 Corinthians 13:4 "Love is neither anxious to impress nor does it cherish inflated ideas of its own importance." (J.B.P.)

Philippians 2:3 "Let nothing be done through strife or vainglory; but in lowliness of mind let each esteem others better than themselves." (KJV)

Matthew 16:24 "Then Jesus said to His disciples, If anyone would come after Me, he must deny himself and take up his cross and follow Me." (NIV)

As you can see, the Bible plainly says **to be honest and deal with our sinful behavior**. We are not to excuse it or blame others. And we certainly are not supposed to sue others who **rightfully** discipline us for bad behavior. Besides, **our value** does not come from **self-inflated statements of love**, but from being forgiven, accepted, and loved by God through Jesus Christ; and that's **eternal value!**

Oh, but these self-love, self-esteem proponents not only twist Scripture and turn a blind eye to the Bible, they also **turn a deaf ear to the facts**. For instance, researchers decided to test the effectiveness of self-esteem teaching in schools by measuring how high the students thought of themselves academically. As it turned out, **the more highly they thought of themselves** and their supposed abilities, **the less ability they had**. A case in point was how kids in Washington D.C. ranked number one in the country for self-esteem. Yet they came in **second to last** in academic performance. One researcher simply stated, "Years of self-love propaganda succeeded only in producing self-deluded kids."[10]

You see, the average person thinks that the teachings of the self-love, self-esteem movement are the antidote needed to cure the wickedness of our world. Yet, in reality, they are actually following the teachings of the king of wickedness, satan.

Isaiah 14:13-14 "You said in your heart, 'I will ascend to heaven; I will raise my throne above the stars of God; I will sit enthroned on the mount of assembly, on the utmost heights of the sacred mountain. I will ascend above the tops of the clouds; I will make myself like the Most High.'" (NIV)

Hmmm. You mean the teaching of man loving and exalting himself above all, even God Himself, started with satan? So is it any wonder that there has been such a massive **Rise of Wickedness**, just like the Bible said? When? In the last days.

The **3rd reason** why people have turned from loving God to loving themselves, causing this **Rise of Wickedness**, is because of the promotion of a **Wicked Witchcraft**. That's right, I'm talking about **wicca**. Little do people know that the teachings of wicca have aided in a **massive rise of wicked behavior**. And for those of you who may not now know, wicca is the modern term for old-fashioned witchcraft. Now, call it what you will; their teachings and practices are not only demonic, but they have **already infiltrated our thinking**.

For instance, witchcraft believes that the entire earth is a living, breathing organism and is the manifestation of the mother goddess. Kind of sounds like environmentalism, doesn't it? Witchcraft says that the mother or female goddess is to be worshipped above all, not a male god. Kind of sounds like feminism, doesn't it? They also say that truth is what is true for you. There are no absolutes. Kind of sounds like relativism, doesn't it? Witchcraft says that in order to contact these gods and goddesses for personal power you need to practice astrology, divination, incantations, psychic power, and speaking with the dead.[11] This kind of sounds like several TV programs **today**, such as "Psychic Hotline" or "Crossing Over" with John Edwards, who supposedly can contact your deceased loved one.

Now, as you guys can see, our society has **already been infiltrated** by the teachings of witchcraft. And thanks to movies and shows like "Charmed" and books like the Harry Potter series, witchcraft has a whole new look; **even for kids**. In fact, it's not only appealing to kids, environmentalists, and feminists but now even to psychologists, who are starting to use witchcraft's occult techniques to treat their patients.[12] In fact, because wicca is now recognized as an "official" religion, the United States Army has allowed approximately one hundred witches to have their own covens at Fort Hood in Texas.[13]

Then, as if that wasn't bad enough, one of the male deities that is worshipped by those in wicca is the "horned god" called Pan. In the ancient cult of Pan, the rites of passage included the use of drugs to entice the "spirits" to come. If someone was possessed by Pan, from which we get the word "panic," it often resulted in an obsession with sex and the need for immediate gratification. And little do people know that Pan is the universal symbol for satan and the antichrist![14]

Because of this slick new campaign presented by witchcraft, wicca is now considered by some to be the **fastest growing religion in the U.S.** and the second most popular religion among teens.[15] And what most people don't realize is that the Bible foretold a time when witchcraft and their demonic practices of sorcery would one day become **commonplace worldwide**.

Revelation 9:20-21 "But the people who did not die in these plagues still refused to turn from their evil deeds. They continued to worship demons and idols made of gold, silver, bronze, stone, and wood – idols that neither see nor hear nor walk! And they did not repent of their murders or their witchcraft or their immorality or their thefts." (NLT)

What? People practicing witchcraft worldwide? Could that really happen? It's already happening before our eyes, just like the Bible said. When? In the last days.

And believe it or not, even with all this amazing evidence pointing to the signs of Christ's soon return, some people still refuse to listen to any kind of godly message, like this lady:

"Two Church members were going door to door sharing God's message of love to be saved and knocked on the door of a woman who was not happy to see them. She told them in no uncertain terms that she did not want to hear their message, and slammed the door in their faces.

To her surprise, however, the door did not close and, in fact, bounced back open. So she tried again, really put her back into it, and slammed the door again with the same result, the door bounced back open.

Convinced that these rude young people were sticking their foot in the door, she reared back to give it a slam that would teach them a lesson, when one of them said, 'Ma'am, before you do that again, you might want to move your cat.'"[16]

Now, that lady caused a lot of unnecessary pain by refusing to listen to God's message, didn't she? But believe it or not, she's not alone. The Bible said that in the last days, many people also refuse to listen to God's message to be saved before it's too late.

2 Corinthians 6:2 "For God says, 'At just the right time, I heard you. On the day of salvation, I helped you.' Indeed, God is ready to help you right now. Today is the day of salvation." (NLT)

People of God, I hope you're not one of those who are refusing to listen to God's message to be saved. Now is the time. Today is the day of salvation.

Why? Because you might wake up one day and discover that **you've been left behind**. And do you know what? God doesn't want you left behind. Because He loves you and I, He has given us the warning sign of **The Rise of Wickedness** to show us that the Tribulation could be near and that Christ's 2nd Coming is rapidly approaching. Jesus Himself said this:

Luke 21:28 "When these things begin to take place, stand up and lift up your heads, because your redemption is drawing near." (NIV)

Like it or not folks, we are headed for **The Final Countdown**. We don't know the day or the hour. Only God knows. The point is, if you're a Christian and you're not going to shoot at the enemy satan, so to speak, then will you at least carry bullets for those who will? Let's roll! Folks, it's high time we Christians speak up and declare the good news of salvation to those who are dying all around us. But please, if you're not a Christian, give your life to Jesus today, because tomorrow may be too late! Just like the Bible said!

Study Questions

Review

Can you remember the signs already mentioned in the Final Countdown book?

Sign #10 was _____ _____ _____

Sign #9 was _____ _____

Sign #8 was _____ _____

Sign #7 was the _____ of _____ __

- As it concerns a rise of falsehood, in what two areas did Jesus say that there would be an increase?

Answer: We would see an increase of:

_____ _____ and

_____ _____

This Chapter:

The #6 Sign on The Final Countdown is none other than the

_____ of _____ .

The 1st End Time Prophecy concerning the rise of wickedness is that people would _____ more than _____ .

2 Timothy 3:1-5 states, "But mark this: there will be terrible times in the last days. People will be *lovers of themselves*, lovers of money, boastful, proud, abusive, disobedient to their parents, ungrateful, unholy, without love, unforgiving, slanderous, without self-control, brutal, not lovers of the good, treacherous, rash, conceited, lovers of pleasure rather than lovers of God— having a form of godliness but denying its power. Have nothing to do with them."

- What is the root of all this wicked behavior?

Answer: it "stems from a _____ ____ _____ instead of a

_____ for _____."

Pastor Billy shared with us 18 wicked fruits of a society that loves itself more than it loves God.

1. Violent crimes are up 995%.

2. The inmate population has grown from about 200,000 to about 2 million.

3. Unmarried couples living together are up 725%.

4. Illegitimate births are up 400%.

5. The divorce rate is now 60%.

6. In some parts of California the rate of divorce is one for every marriage.

7. A murder occurs every 23 minutes.

8.   A rape occurs every 6 minutes.

9.   An aggravated assault occurs every 48 seconds.

10.   An abortion takes place every 20 seconds.

11.   A burglary occurs every 8 seconds.

12.   Sexually transmitted diseases among 10-14 yr. olds are up 385%.

13.   Unwed pregnancies among 10-14 yr. olds are up 553%.

14.   Teenage suicide is up 200%.

15.   The national average of SAT scores has dropped 80 points.

16.   Across America, 25% of graduating seniors couldn't read their diploma.

17.   Every day 13 youth commit suicide, 16 are murdered, 1,000 become mothers, 100,000 bring guns to school, 2,200 drop-out of school, 500 begin using drugs, 1,000 begin drinking alcohol, 3,500 are assaulted, 630 are robbed, and 80 are raped.

18.   More people have died in America in the last 30 years from murders and suicides then from all the wars in the history of the United States.

•   Have any of these fruits of the enemy been growing on the trees close to your personal world?

- What can the church do today to take over our streets and neighborhoods for Christ?

Discussion:

Why have people turned from loving God to loving themselves?

The 1st Reason is because of the promotion of a

_____ _____, _____**which is also called**

_____.

Humanism is the worldview where _____ is the center of all things,

not _____.

Note a few of their own statements of belief from the Humanist Manifesto I and II:

1. Faith in the prayer-hearing God, assumed to live and care for persons, to hear and understand their prayers, and to be able to do something about them, is an unproved and outmoded faith.

2. We find insufficient evidence for the belief in the existence of a supernatural. We begin with humans not God.

3. We do not accept as true the literal interpretation of the Old and New Testaments.

4. We include recognition of an individual's right to die with dignity, euthanasia, suicide, birth control and abortion.

5. We believe that intolerant attitudes, often cultivated by orthodox religions and puritanical cultures, unduly repress sexual conduct. Divorce should be recognized. The many varieties of sexual exploration should not themselves be considered evil.

6. We oppose any tyranny over the mind of man to shackle free thought. In the past such tyrannies have been directed by churches and states attempting to enforce the edicts of religious bigots.

7. Promises of immortal salvation or fear of eternal damnation are both illusory and harmful.

8. Salvationism, based on mere affirmation, still appears as harmful, diverting people with false hopes of heaven hereafter. No deity will save us; we must save ourselves.

- Under the premise that religion and education don't mix, what did the humanists force out of our schools?

Answer: The _____, _____, and the

_____ _____.

- When did the Supreme Court consider humanism a religion?

Answer: Back in the early _____.

- Whose "religious" teachings are filling our school without even being questioned?

Answer: _____

The following are some quotes by some of history's leaders of humanism:

_____ _____ **(1803-1876)** boldly stated,

"(Our) great object was to get rid of _____, and to convert

our churches into halls of _____. The plan was not to make open attacks on religion...but to establish a system of state schools, from which all religion was to be excluded...and to which all parents were to be compelled by law to send their children. For this purpose, a secret society was formed and the whole country was to be organized."

_____ _____ **(1796-1858)**

"What the church has been for medieval man, the _____

_____ must become for democratic and rational man.

God would be _____ by the concept of the public good."

_____ _____ **(1859-1952)**

"There is _____ God and there is no soul. Hence, there is no need for the props of traditional religion. With dogma and creed excluded, then immutable truth is also dead and buried. There is no room for fixed, natural law or moral _____."

Charles F. Potter Humanism: A New Religion (1930)

"Education is thus a most powerful _____ of humanism, and _____

American school is a school of _____. What can a theistic Sunday School's meeting for an hour once a week and teaching only a fraction of the children do to stem the tide of the five-day program of humanistic teaching?"

Paul Blanshard, 1976

"Our schools may not teach Johnny to read properly, but the fact that Johnny is in school until he is sixteen tends to lead toward the

_____ of religious _____."

G. Richard Bozarth wrote in "American Atheist", November 1977

"We must ask how we can _____ the God of Christianity. We need only to insure that our schools teach only _____ knowledge. If we could achieve this, God would indeed be shortly due for a funeral service."

John J. Dunphy January/February 1983

"The classroom must and will become an arena of conflict between the old and the new – the rotting corpse of Christianity...and the new faith of humanism."

The average person today thinks that the teachings of humanism are the

_____ needed to cure the wickedness of the world. Yet,

Pastor Billy reminds us that, "in reality they are actually _____

the teachings of the King of wickedness, _____. Read Genesis 3:4-5

The 2nd Reason why people have turned from loving God to loving themselves, causing a rise of wickedness is because of the promotion of a

_____ _____; also referred to as the _____

_____ and _____ - _____ movement.

Two psychologists, especially responsible for this explosion of self-worship

are Abraham _____ and Carl _____.

They have convinced multitudes that we must love ourselves at all cost, even

if it means _____ sinful behavior, _____

from discipline, _____ others, and _____ personal

_____.

They say that if we force people to deal with their own wicked behavior then we

will _____ their self-esteem.

Even preachers have come to that famous passage in Matthew 22:37-39 and

twisted it so it fits in with the self-esteem teaching. It reads, "Jesus replied, "you

must love the Lord your God with all your heart, all your soul, and all

your mind. "This is the _____and greatest commandment. A

_____ is equally important: Love your neighbor as yourself."

- What are the two commands He gave?

Answer: Love _____ and Love _____ _____

Yet many add a 3rd commandment to _____ _____.

The reasoning goes like this: "Unless you love yourself first, you won't have the ability to love God or your neighbor."

- But what caused the fall of man?

Answer: Loving _____ more than _____.

Note the obvious passages in the Bible that teach _____

to love yourself, but instead exhort us to deal honestly with our sin.

Ezekiel 20:43 "There you will remember your conduct and all the actions by which you have defiled yourselves, and *you will loathe yourselves* for all the evil you have done."

Romans 7:18, 24 "I know that nothing good lives in me, that is, in my sinful nature. *What a wretched man I am*! Who will rescue me from this body of death?"

Ezekiel 36:31-32 "Then you will remember your evil ways and wicked deeds, and *you will loathe yourselves* for your sins and detestable practices. Be ashamed and disgraced for your conduct, O House of Israel!"

Job 42:6 "Therefore *I despise myself* and repent in dust and ashes."

2 Corinthians 5:15 "And he died for all, that those who live *should no longer live for themselves* but for him who died for them and was raised again."

Luke 6:32-33,35 "If you love those who love you, what credit is that to you? Even 'sinners' love those who love them. And if you do good to those who are good to you, what credit is that to you? Even 'sinners' do that. But *love your enemies*, do good to them, and lend to them without expecting to get anything back."

1 Corinthians 13:4 "Love is neither anxious to impress *nor does it cherish inflated ideas of its own importance*."

Matthew 16:24 "Then Jesus said to His disciples, If anyone would come after Me, *he must deny himself* and take up his cross and follow Me."

- If our value doesn't come from self-inflated statements of love, from where does it come, as Christians?

Answer: From being _____ , _____, and

_____ by God through Jesus Christ.

Self-love, self-esteem proponents not only twists Scripture, but they also turn a deaf ear to the facts.

Researchers decided to test the effectiveness of self-esteem teaching in schools. One would think that the more highly one thought of himself/herself, the higher they would do academically. But the opposite was true.

As it turned out, the more highly they thought of themselves and their

supposed abilities, the _____ ability they had." (e.g. Kids in

Washington DC ranked #1 in the country for self-esteem; yet they came

second to _____ in academic performance.)

- What have 'years of self-love propaganda succeeded in producing?

Answer: _____ _____ kids.

A 3rd Reason why people have turned from loving God to loving themselves, causing this rise of wickedness is because of the promotion of a

_____ _____, also referred to as _____.

Wicca is the modern term for old-fashioned witchcraft.

Note how Wicca has already infiltrated our thinking:

It believes that the entire earth is a living, breathing organism and a manifestation of the mother goddess.

Sounds like _____.

It believes that the mother or female goddess is to be worshiped above all, not a male god.

Sounds like _____.

It believes that truth is what is true for you.

Sounds like _____.

It believes that in order to contact these gods and goddesses for personal

power, you need to practice _____, _____ ,

_____, _____ power, and speaking with the

_____.

> Sounds like those TV programs today like "Psychic Hotline", or "Crossing Over" with John Edwards

- What are psychologists today starting to use to treat their patients?

Answer: _____ _____ _____

Because Wicca is recognized as an "official" religion, the US Army has allowed around _____ witches to have their own covens at Fort Hood in Texas.

One of the male deities worshiped by Wiccans is the "horned god" called _____. Anyone possessed by Pan was obsessed with _____ and the need for immediate _____. Pan is the universal symbol for _____ and the _____.

- The Bible foretold a time when witchcraft and its demonic practices of sorcery would one day become commonplace _____;

Revelation 9:20-21 tells us; "But the people who did not die in these plagues still refused to turn from their evil deeds. They continued to worship demons and idols made of gold, silver, bronze, stone, and wood – idols that neither see nor hear nor walk! And they did not repent of their murders or their witchcraft or their immorality or their thefts."

Jesus Christ is soon, very soon, coming back! Are you ready to meet Him face to face?

The 6th sign of a Rise of Wickedness is a great encouragement to God's people.

Jesus declared in Luke 21:28, "When these things begin to take place, stand up and lift up your heads, because your redemption is drawing near."

God's Day is drawing near. It is time to get right with God the Father through His Son Jesus Christ.

Chapter Six

The Rise of Apostasy

"One day a man entered a cafe and sat down to get something to eat, when he notices that the special of the day is cold chili. When the waitress comes to take his order, he says, 'I'll take the cold chili.'

'I'm sorry, the gentleman next to you got the last bowl,' replied the waitress.

'Oh, I'll just have coffee, then.'

But after a while the man notices that the guy next to him who got the last bowl of cold chili was finishing a rather large meal and the chili bowl he ordered was just sitting there, still full.

So he asked, 'Are you going to eat that?'

The other man replied, 'No.'

'Would you sell it to me?'

The other man said, 'You can have it for free if you want it.'

So the man takes the bowl of chili with lots of nice big chunks in it and begins to eat it. But as he got about half way through the bowl, he notices a dead mouse in the bowl and pukes the chili back into the bowl.

And the other man said sympathetically, 'Yeah, that's about as far as I got, too.'"[1]

Now, that guy's situation went from **bad to worse real fast** didn't it? But did you know that one of these days, many people's lives all over the earth will also go from bad to worse; except it won't be from a bowl of bad chili. It's going to be from a **bowl of God's wrath** poured out upon a wicked and rebellious planet. You see, because people refuse to get right with God through Jesus Christ they are sadly running the risk of being left behind. And if that wasn't bad enough, it's going to get even worse real fast when they discover that they've been catapulted into the seven-year Tribulation that is coming upon the whole world.

And folks, the time of the Tribulation is not a party. Jesus said in **Matthew 24** that it would be a time of greater horror than anything the world has ever seen or will ever see again. He also said that unless that time of calamity is shortened, the entire human race would be destroyed. But God is not only a God of wrath; He's a God of love as well. And **because He loves you and I**, He has given us many warning signs so that we would know when the Tribulation could be near and that Christ's 2nd Coming is rapidly approaching. Therefore, to make sure our lives don't go from bad to worse by being left behind, we're going to continue taking a look at **The Final Countdown**.

We already saw how the **#10** sign on **The Final Countdown** was **The Jewish People**. The #9 sign was **Modern Technology**. The #8 sign was **Worldwide Upheaval**. The #7 sign was **The Rise of Falsehood**. And last time we saw that the #6 sign was none other than **The Rise of Wickedness**. There we saw that God lovingly foretold you and I that when we see an increase of people loving themselves more than God, which is occurring **today** through humanism, self-love self-esteem, and witchcraft, that this would be an indicator that we are in the last days.

But that's not the only signs that God has given us. The **#5** sign on **The Final Countdown** is none other than **The Rise of Apostasy**. So just what are these specific prophesies being fulfilled today concerning **The Rise of Apostasy**, revealing that we could be in the last days? Well, I'm glad you asked. Let's take a look. The **1ˢᵗ End Time Prophecy** concerning **The Rise of Apostasy** is that **people would deliberately turn away from the truth**.

1 Timothy 4:1-2 "Now the Holy Spirit tells us clearly that in the last times some will turn away from what we believe; they will follow lying spirits and teachings that come from demons. These teachers are hypocrites and liars. They pretend to be religious, but their consciences are dead." (NLT)

According to this passage of Scripture, one of the major characteristics of the Church in the last days is that many people will pretend to be religious and give the appearance of being Christians. Yet will show their true colors by turning away from the truth to follow hypocritical teachings. Now, throughout history we've always had some people following perverted truths of Christianity. That's been commonplace. But what's **not common** is how, **in the last century alone**, there has been a **mass exodus** of people claiming to be Christians who have turned away from even the basic truths of Christianity. And it's only getting worse. There has been a tremendous change in the attitude, behavior, and beliefs of those in the Church here in America as recently as the last fifteen years. Today we have people in the Church who don't even bat an eye, saying such things as, "Jesus sinned just like us," or "It doesn't matter what religion you follow, they all teach the same thing," or "There is no such place as hell," or even "The devil is not a real being but rather a mere symbol of evil." Don't believe me? Let me show you just how bad it's become. Let's take a look at the change of beliefs of those who are "claiming" to be Christians here in America in **just the last 15 years**.

1. 80% of Christians believe "the Bible teaches that God helps those who help themselves."
2. 53% says the Holy Spirit does not exist.
3. 12% do not know what will happen to them after they die.
4. 25% agreed that it doesn't matter what faith you follow because all faith groups teach the same lessons.
5. 30% says that Jesus Christ died but never had a physical resurrection.
6. 29% contend that "when he lived on earth, Jesus Christ was human and committed sins, like other people."
7. 29% assert that "there are some crimes, sins, or other things which people might do which cannot be forgiven by God."
8. 47% says that satan does not exist.
9. 22% agreed that all people will experience the same outcomes after death, regardless of their religious beliefs.
10. 31% says that a good person can earn his/her way into heaven.[2]

Now, I don't know about you guys, but **in the last 15 years alone**, it sure sounds like there's been a massive **Rise of Apostasy**, hasn't there? Just like the Bible said. When? In the last days.

But the question is, "How could there be such a mass exodus of people deliberately turning from the basic truths of Christianity in such a short amount of time, especially in America which boasts of being a Christian nation? Great question. I'm glad you asked. The **1ˢᵗ reason** why people **in the Church** have turned from the truth to follow hypocritical teachings, causing this **Rise of Apostasy**, is by a focus on **Marketing Madness**. That's right, I'm talking about the **Church Growth Movement**. Little do people know that the teachings of the Church Growth Movement have actually aided in this **massive rise of apostasy**. Today, people **in the Church** are being led astray by **marketing manipulation**. They are being told that true spiritual Christians need to utilize worldly marketing techniques in order to have any kind of Church growth. **But the catch** is that, in order to do this, one needs to adopt an attitude of **compromise with the Scripture**. How's that? Well, let's find out by looking at a comparison of **just a few** of their teachings verses that of the Bible:

Church Growth Teachings vs. the Bible

1. CGM: The primary goal of the Church is numerical growth.
    Bible: The primary goal of the Church is spiritual growth. (Ephesians 4:11-16)

2. CGM: The Pastor's primary role is as an encourager who makes people feel good.
    Bible: The Pastor's primary role is as a teacher. (Ephesians 4:11)

3. CGM: The style of music is to be what the culture likes and is pleasing to them.
    Bible: The style of music is to be from the heart and what is glorifying to God. (Ephesians 5:19)

4. CGM: The means of evangelism is to use marketing techniques to draw people in instead of going out into the community.
    Bible: The means of evangelism is to go into all the world making disciples and not just wait for them to come to you. (Matthew 28:19-20)

5. CGM: Sermons should only contain positive messages and not negative ones about hell or God's wrath and hatred towards sin.
    Bible: Sermons are to preach the whole counsel of God not just part of it. (2 timothy 4:2)[3]

Now, as you can see, the basic teachings of the Church Growth Movement are completely antithetical to the Scripture. And you might think that nobody in the Church would ever fall for this wacky stuff. Yet, it has now become the latest craze in "running a Church." But sadly, because people are now promoting worldly marketing techniques as opposed to the clear teaching of the Word of God, many Christians are **not growing spiritually**, **many Churches**

are splitting, and even non-Christians are being presented with a **false gospel**. And all for the sake of numbers. The culture is now to dictate proper behavior to the Church instead of the Church dictating to the culture. This has given rise to a cultural Christianity instead of Christ-like Christianity. Now, I know this might be hard to believe, but did you know that the Apostle Paul was able to share the gospel and plant Church after Church without utilizing one marketing technique to draw people in? In fact, he purposely **went out into communities** to evangelize, and all this **without** a Christian rock band. His method was simple: **he simply relied on the power of the gospel**.

1 Corinthians 1:17-19 "For Christ didn't send me to baptize, but to preach the Good News – and not with clever speeches and high-sounding ideas, for fear that the cross of Christ would lose its power.

I know very well how foolish the message of the cross sounds to those who are on the road to destruction. But we who are being saved recognize this message as the very power of God. As the Scriptures say, 'I will destroy human wisdom and discard their most brilliant ideas.'" (NLT)

Hmmm. You mean that one day people **in the Church** would actually be led astray into apostasy by **false methodologies from the world that would actually be powerless to save people**? That would be, **uh huh**. So is it any wonder that there's been a massive **Rise of Apostasy** just like the Bible said? When? In the last days.

The **2nd reason** why people **in the Church** have turned from the truth to follow hypocritical teachings, causing this **Rise of Apostasy**, is by a focus on **Money and Materialism**. That's right, I'm talking about the **Word of Faith Movement**. Little do people know that the teachings of the Word of Faith Movement have actually aided in this **massive rise of apostasy**. Today, people **in the Church** are being led astray by **monetary manipulation**. In fact, they would say that if you **just have enough faith**, you could obtain untold riches from God. But don't just take my word for it, let's listen to some of their most prominent leaders:

ACTUAL STATEMENTS FROM WORD OF FAITH TEACHERS

1. **Kenneth Copeland:** "satan conquered Jesus on the cross."
2. **Morris Cerullo:** "You're not looking at Morris Cerullo – you're looking at God. You're looking at Jesus."
3. **Benny Hinn:** "Never, ever, ever go to the Lord and say, 'If it be thy will…' Don't allow such faith destroying words to be spoken from your mouth."
4. **Frederick Price:** "God has to be given permission to work in this earth realm on behalf of man…Yes! You are in control! So if man has control, who no longer has it? God."
5. **Benny Hinn:** "Adam could fly like a bird, swim underwater like a fish, and even transport himself to the moon."
6. **Kenneth Hagin:** "Because Jesus was recreated from a satanic being to an incarnation of God, you too can become an incarnation – as much an incarnation as Jesus Christ of Nazareth."
7. **Kenneth Copeland:** "Your word is God's command."
8. **Jerry Savelle:** "By using your tongue to release the force of faith, you can speak whatsoever you desire into existence."
9. **John Avanzini:** "Jesus was wealthy and prosperous. He lived in a big house, handled big money, and even wore designer clothes.[4]

Now, as you can see, the basic teachings of the Word of Faith Movement are not only completely antithetical to the Scripture, but they are **manipulating people** by promising false techniques to obtain so-called fabulous wealth. You see, the catch is that you have to send them **your money** to get these supposedly **free** financial blessings from God. In exchange for sowing a seed, a financial one that is, they will send you the latest religious trinket to help you get rich. For instance, to acquire these untold riches, right now you can send off for a genuine faith nail, prayer cloth, prayer candle, paper prayer rug, anointing oil, and that's right, a cornmeal miracle packet.[5] And when you follow the secret formula on how to pray for your financial blessing, these people promise to personally pray for a one hundred fold increase, to your **generous donation** into their ministry, of course.

Now, you might think that nobody **in the Church** would fall for this wacky stuff. Yet **right now**, there are shelves full of this stuff in every Christian bookstore, promising not only financial blessings but **spiritual blessings as well**. But the catch is, in order for you to utilize these secret prayers or formulas which are guaranteed to bring you that blessing, you **first** have to **buy their book**. Just who's getting rich here? And these faith ministries are raking in millions of dollars each year off of people **seeking, not Christ, but cash**! The sad thing is that they are giving the world the false idea that God is merely some kind of a "Cosmic Santa Claus," or a "Golden Genie" who, if we rub with the right methodology, **has to give us** whatever we wish. One man talks about this "new Jesus" that has appeared on the scene:

"The function of God has been changed. He has a whole new role. No longer is He the object of all worship and adoration. Instead He has become an important means for getting what we now worship and adore—things, or at least the money to buy the things. In our brave new world we worship the things we have been conditioned to want, and we will be religious if religion can guarantee us the products our democratic capitalistic society turns out by the tons.

This new Jesus propagates a 'prosperity theology' that promises the faithful if they seek first the kingdom of this reconstructed deity and do all the things the pop religious books say will guarantee success, then all these things (the ones described in the ads) will be added unto them. This is a new religion that is functional, fit for these new believers who hunger for consumer goods. It has, as they say, 'user-friendly churches' that are just right for people whose God is a super-genie who can be at our beck and call through prayer and who will help us succeed in life…which of course means to get all the things we don't need, so as to gratify our media-created hungers.

From time to time, a person comes along and reminds us of the other Jesus. We admire her and Him. But then we hurry back to that real Jesus who doesn't demand sacrifices for the poor and oppressed but simply promises to be there to help us, as the ad for the army suggests, all that we can be."[6]

Folks, God is not at our beck and call. He is God and we are not. And what the Word of Faith Movement has done is to turn God into a mere force that supposedly can be tapped into by faith to satisfy our lust for **personal gain**! Besides, I know this might be hard to believe, but the Apostle Peter was profoundly used by God, and to my knowledge, he never once owned an Armani suit or even drove a single Cadillac. In fact, there's no record of him chanting an Old Testament prayer over and over again in order to increase his ministry. However, Peter **did warn us** about this kind of monetary manipulation **in the Church** that would come in the last days.

2 Peter 2:1,3 "But there were also false prophets in Israel, just as there will be false teachers among you. In their greed they will make up clever lies to get hold of your money. But God condemned them long ago, and their destruction is on the way." (NLT)

Hmmm. You mean that in the last days that people **in the Church** would actually be led astray into apostasy by **false teachers ripping people off by promising fabulous wealth**? That would be, **uh huh**. So is it any wonder that there's been a massive **Rise of Apostasy** just like the Bible said? When? In the last days.

The **3rd reason** why people **in the Church** have turned from the truth to follow hypocritical teachings, causing this **Rise of Apostasy**, is by a focus on **Magnificent Miracles**. That's right, I'm talking about the **Signs and Wonders Movement**. Little do people know that the teachings of the Signs and Wonders Movement have actually aided in this **massive rise of apostasy**. Today, people **in the Church** are being led astray by **emotional manipulation**. We are being told that true spiritual growth can only come from having a **new** experience or **new** emotional encounter with God. Such things as ecstatic speech, barking like dogs, having convulsions, or even uncontrollable laughter, are now the **new signs** of true spiritual maturity and a genuine encounter with God. Yet what most people **in the Church** don't realize is that these supposedly new spiritual experiences are not only **not Scriptural**, but they're actually strikingly similar to **old-fashioned occultic behavior**. See for yourself:

SIGNS & WONDERS EXPERIENCES vs. THE OCCULT

<u>Signs & Wonders</u>	<u>Hindu Gurus</u>	<u>Meditation</u>	<u>African Spiritism</u>
1. Slain in the spirit	√	√	√
2. Electrical shock	√	√	√
3. Physical jerks	√	√	√
4. Animal sounds	√	√	√
5. New revelations	√	√	√
6. Surge of energy	√	√	√
7. Ecstatic speech	√	√	√
8. Trances	√	√	√
9. Visions	√	√	√
10. Uncontrollable laughing	√	√	√[7]

Apparently, this kind of behavior isn't so new after all. There might be a "spirit" behind these so-called "spiritual experiences," but I don't see it as being consistent with the Spirit of God. Now, as you guys can see, people **in the Church** are sadly being emotionally manipulated into thinking that they are having an encounter with God, when in reality they are having **an encounter with occultic practices**. And I know this might be hard to believe, but to my knowledge, the early Church was able to grow like wildfire, and yet they never once broke out into uncontrollable laughter or even made animal noises. Besides, little do people know that through these false signs and wonders, people are actually being prepared **to be deceived** by the ultimate false miracle worker, the antichrist.

2 Thessalonians 2:8-9 "And then the lawless one will be revealed, whom the Lord Jesus will overthrow with the breath of his mouth and destroy by the splendor of his coming. The coming of the lawless one will be in accordance with the work of satan displayed in all kinds of counterfeit miracles, signs and wonders." (NIV)

Hmmm. You mean that in the last days, people **in the Church** would be led astray into apostasy by **false signs and wonders**, which will also be used by the antichrist? That would be, **uh huh**. So is it any wonder that there's been a massive **Rise of Apostasy** just like the Bible said? When? In the last days.

The **4th reason** why people have turned from the truth to follow hypocritical teachings, causing this **Rise of Apostasy**, is by a focus on **Making My Own Doctrine**. That's right, I'm talking about the **Liberal Christianity Movement**. Little do people know that the teachings of Liberalism have actually aided in this **massive rise of apostasy**. Today, people are being led astray by **doctrinal manipulation**.

And for those of you who may not know, Liberal Christianity is not true Christianity. Like a wolf in sheep's clothing, it externally looks Christian, when in fact, internally they actually **doctrinally manipulate** almost every cardinal teaching of the Church. For instance, they not only deny the deity, miracles, and resurrection of Christ, but they go so far as to say that true and loving Christians will have an **open mind** when it comes to understanding the Bible. They say that **feelings**, not doctrine, provide the foundation for Christianity. Or in other words, your version of Christianity is what feels right for you. In essence, **you make up your own doctrine**.

Now, you might think that nobody **in the Church** would fall for this kind of wacky stuff. But why do you think that, **right now**, mainline denominations are battling over whether or not Jesus really is the only way to heaven? Or, why do you think that many people claiming to be Christians are actually denying the existence of hell? Or, why do you think that many so-called Churches have not only accepted homosexuality as a positive lifestyle, but now say it's okay even for those behind the pulpit? I'll tell you why. It's all because they are manipulating doctrine to suit their own sinful fancies. Oh, but they're not only making up their own doctrine, they're making up their own version of the Bible. You see, just to make sure that nobody **runs the risk of being offended by the truth**, liberals have started to pervert the actual text of the Bible. Here, see for yourself with a sample of some of the "new" versions out there:

The Politically Correct Version:

Referring to the Oxford University Press's release of a 'culturally sensitive' version of the Bible, the religious editor of *Newsweek* recently quipped that the King James Bible 'never looked so good before.' These are his poignant comments:

Readers who find the Bible sexist, racist, elitist and insensitive to the physically challenged, take heart. Oxford University Press's new 'inclusive language version' of the New Testament and Psalms has cleaned up God's act. In this version, God is no longer 'Father' and Jesus is no longer 'Son.'

The hierarchical title of 'Lord' is excised as an archaic way to address God. Nor does God (male pronouns for the deity have been abolished) rule a 'kingdom'; as the editors explain, the word has a 'blatantly androcentric and patriarchal character.'...Even God's metaphorical 'right hand' has been amputated out of deference to the left-handed. Some examples:

- In the majestic opening of John's Gospel, 'the glory he has from the Father as the only Son of the Father' becomes 'the glory as of a parent's only child.' (John 1:14)

- The Lord's prayer now begins like this: 'Father-Mother, hallowed be your name. May your dominion come.' (Luke 11:2)

- Jesus' own self-understanding as God's only son is generalized to: 'No one knows the Child except the Father-Mother; and no one knows the Father-Mother except the Child...' (Matthew 11:27)

- Avoiding another traditional phrase, 'Son of Man,' the Oxford text reads: 'Then they will see 'the Human One' coming in clouds with great power and glory.' (Mark 13:26)

The editors do not claim that Jesus spoke in gender-neutral language. But they obviously think he should have. The changes they have made are not merely cosmetic. They represent a fundamental reinterpretation of what the New Testament says—and how it says it."

The New Feminist Version:

A publisher is touting a new edition of the Gospels that identifies Christ as a woman named Judith Christ of Nazareth. LBI Institute says its version, was needed to correct the gender of Christ and God

'This long-awaited revised text of the Gospels makes the moral message of Christ more accessible to many, and more illuminating to all,' says Billie Shakespeare, vice president for the publisher. He said, 'It is empowering. We published this new Bible to acknowledge the rise of women in society.'

The new version, according to the publisher, revises familiar stories, transforming the 'Prodigal Son' into the 'Prodigal Daughter' and the 'Lord's Prayer' into the 'Lady's Prayer.' Here are a few other examples of the 'new' translation.

- In Luke chapter 2 the verses now read, 'And Joseph went to Bethlehem. To be enrolled with Mary, his wife, who was then pregnant. And she brought forth her firstborn child. And her name was chosen to be Judith.'

- A passage on the crucifixion, from John 19 says, 'And She bearing her cross went forth. There they crucified Judith.'

- And a resurrection passage from Matthew 28 now states, 'Mary Magdalene and the other Mary came to see the tomb. But the angel said to the women, 'Do not be afraid, for I know that you seek Judith who was crucified. She is not here; for She is risen.''

The New Postmodern Version:

This new version takes Darwin's theory of evolution as gospel and presents Jesus as being born, 'not to a virgin, but to a gorilla.' According to Ruth Rimm, Bronx school teacher and book artist, 'It explores the emergence of a new global spirituality that mixes the best of each wisdom tradition with the latest findings in psychology, quantum physics, neuroscience, and linguistics. It is a Bible for skeptics, seekers, and people of different faiths.'

The first volume in the series, which will eventually present the Torah, Bhagavad Gita, Buddhist sutras, and Sufi mysticism, covers the Gospel of Mark. However, it includes parables not found in Mark, such as the Parable of the Dolphin, the Parable of the Snow Leopard and the Parable of the Gorilla.

The Parable of the Gorilla begins with, 'He was born in a manger a long time ago, not to a virgin, but to a gorilla. What's so funny? Who did you expect his ancestors to look like, Tom Cruise? But wait. I'm not making fun of Jesus. I'm not mocking religion. In fact, from the deepest wellspring of my heart, I'm despairing something we've lost in our scientific culture.

Yes, if Jesus was alive today, he would understand that his ancestors, just like ours, were beasts. No, he wouldn't run around claiming he was born of a virgin. And, brilliant rabbi that he was, he would likely ask us to understand the miracle stories metaphorically, as morality tales, but certainly not as literal truth.'[8]

Now, are those "new" versions of the Bible utter blasphemy or what? So the question is, "Why would anyone dare pervert the Holy Bible? And why is it just the Holy Bible? Why don't they try this with the Jewish Torah or the Muslim Koran?" Well, one of the many reasons why liberals have twisted the Scripture is because they say that the old versions might offend some people and since that wouldn't be **a positive experience** for some, new neutral versions are required. And now it apparently doesn't matter what's right or wrong. Apparently, even though I claim to be a Christian, I don't have to follow Christ's teaching. I now get to follow which commands are pleasing to me, **not Him**. And of course, this means I also get to redefine the terminology for what's considered appropriate behavior. This is precisely what our liberal society has done:

"What our Founding Fathers referred to as drunkenness because of their Christian heritage, we now call it *alcoholism* and deem it a social disease, rather than a sin.

What the Law-Word called sodomy, we now call an *alternative life style*, giving this a political identity and the unassuming name of *gay rights* and *sexual orientation*. Pornography is a perversion that brings death to a nation, and yet we call it *adult entertainment*.

What our Founding Fathers called immorality, we now call it the *new morality*; what the law called adultery or fornication, we now call *stepping out* or *fooling around*; and what the Law called abhorrent social behavior (like stealing or filthy language), we now call *abnormal social development* or *anti-social behavior*."[9]

You see, once you adopt the liberal attitude that says you can't trust the Bible, or worse yet, say that you yourself can interpret the Bible any way you want, you've just opened the floodgates of heresy. And once that happens, the Church will be drowned in apostasy. This is precisely what we see today. And what most people don't realize is that the Bible foretold of a time when people **in the Church**, claiming to be Christians, would not only make up their own doctrine but they would also **deliberately gather around them** liberal teachers to tell them, not the truth, but **what they want to hear**.

2 Timothy 4:3-4 "For a time is coming when people will no longer listen to right teaching. They will follow their own desires and will look for teachers who will tell them whatever they want to hear. They will reject the truth and follow strange myths." (NLT)

What? You mean that in the last days people **in the Church** will be claiming to be Christians yet will knowingly follow lying teachers because they get told what they want to hear? Could that really happen? It's already happening before our eyes, just like the Bible said. When? In the last days.

And believe it or not, even with all this amazing evidence pointing to the signs of Christ's soon return, some people still think that they can mix the good with the bad without having any head problems, like this guy:

"There was a man who was a Buffalo Sabres fan who had a big dilemma. He wanted to marry a lady who was a Toronto Maple Leafs fan. And knowing that this would be a lifelong problem, the Buffalo Sabres fan agreed to have 50% of his brain removed in order to ensure compatibility in the marriage. So he goes to his doctor and says, 'I've just got to marry this woman who's a Toronto Maple Leafs fan. I love her so much.'

So the doctor says, 'Well, it's risky, but okay.'

So into the operating room they go for the brain removal procedure.

Later though, when the man who was the Buffalo Sabres fan woke up, the doctor came in and said, 'We are very sorry, but we accidentally removed 75% of your brain instead of 50%.'

To which the man looked up and said, 'Go Leafs!'"[10]

Now that guy found out the hard way that, try as you might, you can't mix the good with the bad, can you? It not only caused him some serious head problems but his condition even worsened, didn't it? But believe it or not, he's not alone. You see, many people today also think that they can mix hypocritical teachings with Christianity and still be Christians. Yet the Bible says that these "religious" people are sadly in line for the ultimate rude awakening from Jesus Himself.

Matthew 7:21-23 "Not all people who sound religious are really godly. They may refer to me as 'Lord,' but they still won't enter the Kingdom of Heaven. The decisive issue is whether they obey my Father in heaven.

On judgment day many will tell me, 'Lord, Lord, we prophesied in your name and cast out demons in your name and performed many miracles in your name.' But I will reply, 'I never knew you. Go away; the things you did were unauthorized." (NLT)

People of God, I hope you're not one of those who are busy being religious yet have never truly bowed a knee before Jesus Christ. I hope that you have honestly surrendered your life to Him by following **all of His teachings**, not just the ones you like. Why? Because you might wake up one day and discover that **you've been left behind**. And do you know what? God doesn't want you left behind. Because He loves you and I, He has given us the warning sign of **The Rise of Apostasy** to show us that the Tribulation **could be near** and that Christ's 2nd Coming is rapidly approaching. Jesus Himself said this:

Luke 21:28 "When these things begin to take place, stand up and lift up your heads, because your redemption is drawing near." (NIV)

Like it or not folks, we are headed for **The Final Countdown**. We don't know the day or the hour. Only God knows. The point is, if you're a Christian, and you're not willing to go to the front lines to fight for the cause of Christ, then will you at least support those who will? Let's rock! Folks, it's high time we Christians speak up and declare the good news of salvation to those who are dying all around us. But please, if you're not a Christian, give your life to Jesus today, because tomorrow may be too late! Just like the Bible said!

Study Questions

Review

- Jesus Christ's coming again is rapidly approaching. Can you remember, up to this point, the five signs that were studied that confirm His soon return?

Answer: Sign #10 was _____ _____ _____

Sign # 9 was _____ _____

Sign # 8 was _____ _____

Sign #7 was The _____ ___ _____

Sign #6 was The _____ ____ _____

The 'study-in-a-nutshell', in this last chapter, was that God lovingly told us that in the last days before Jesus' 2nd Coming there would be an increase of people loving _____ more than _____. Pastor Billy exposed the three avenues that people today love themselves more than God:

First: Through the religion of _____

Secondly: Through the self-_____, self-_____ movement

Thirdly: Through _____ or _____.

This Chapter:

The #5 Sign on the Final Countdown is none other than the _____ of

_____ .

The Rise of Apostasy means, that in these last days,
people would _____ turn away from the
_____ .

Paul wrote in 1 Timothy 4:1-2, "Now the Holy Spirit tells us clearly that in the last times some will turn away from what we believe; they will follow lying spirits and teachings that come from demons. These teachers are hypocrites and liars. They pretend to be religious, but their consciences are dead."

These verses tell us clearly that "one of the major characteristics of the church in

the last days is that many people will _____ to be religious and give

the _____ of being Christians. Yet will show their true colors by

_____ _____ from the _____ to follow hypocritical

_____

- Today, what bold statements have people in the Church made?

Answer:

"Jesus _____ just like us."

"It _____ matter what religion you follow, they all teach the

_____ thing,"

"There is no such place as _____ ."

"The devil is not a _____ being but rather a mere _____ of evil.

Let's note some of the "change of beliefs" claimed by "Christians" in American Churches in just the last 15 years:

1. Eighty percent of Christians believe "the Bible teaches that God helps those who help themselves."

2. Fifty three percent say the Holy Spirit does not exist.

3. Twelve percent do not know what will happen to them after they die.

4. Twenty five percent agreed that it doesn't matter what faith you follow because all faith groups teach the same lessons.

5. Thirty percent say that Jesus Christ died but never had a physical resurrection.

6. Twenty nine percent contend that "when he lived on earth, Jesus Christ was human and committed sins, like other people."

7. Twenty nine percent assert that "there are some crimes, sins, or other things which people might do which cannot be forgiven by God."

8. Forty seven percent say that satan does not exit.

9. Twenty two percent agreed that all people will experience the same outcomes after death, regardless of their religious beliefs.

10. Thirty one percent say that a good person can earn his/her way into Heaven.

There are two reasons for such a mass exodus of people deliberately abandoning the basic truths of Christianity.

THE 1ST REASON PEOPLE HAVE APOSTATIZED TODAY - A FOCUS ON _____ AND _____ (OR TO PUT IT IN OTHER TERMS) THE _____ OF _____

_____.

• How are people in the church being led astray by this movement?

Answer: By _____ manipulation.

They would say that if you just have enough _____, you could obtain untold _____ from God.

Listen to some actual statements from some of Word of Faith's most prominent leaders:

1. **Kenneth Copeland**: "satan conquered Jesus on the cross."

2. **Morris Cerullo**: "You're not looking at Morris Cerullo-you're looking at God. You're looking at Jesus."

3. **Benny Hinn**: Never, ever, ever go the Lord and say, 'If it be thy will…' Don't allow such faith destroying words to be spoken from your mouth."

4. **Frederick Price**: "God has to be given permission to work in this earth realm on behalf of man…Yes! You are in control! So if man has control, who no longer has it? God."

5. **Benny Hinn**: "Adam could fly like a bird, swim underwater like a fish, and even transport himself to the moon.

6. **Kenneth Hagin**: "Because Jesus was recreated from a satanic being to an incarnation of God, you too can become an incarnation – as much an incarnation as Jesus Christ of Nazareth."

7. **Kenneth Copeland**: "Your word is God's command."

8. **Jerry Savelle**: "By using your tongue to release the force of faith, you can speak whatsoever you desire into existence."

9. **John Avanzini**: "Jesus was wealthy and prosperous. He lived in a big house, handled big money, and even wore designer clothes.

- What do these leaders and many more do it manipulate people into thinking that they'll be fabulously wealthy?

Answer: You have to send them your _____ to get these supposedly _____ financial blessings from God.

- What will these Word of Faith leaders send you, if you 'sow a seed', a financial seed of course?

Answer: They will send you the latest religious _____ to help you get _____ .

Let's note some of these magical trinkets:

    ✓ a genuine faith _____ .

    ✓ a prayer _____ .

    ✓ a prayer _____ .

    ✓ a _____ prayer rug.

    ✓ _____ oil.

    ✓ a _____ miracle packet.

These church leaders promise to personally pray for a 100-fold increase in your life for your _____ donation to their ministry.

- Who is really getting rich?

Answer: (We'll let you answer that one!)

One man talks about this "new Jesus" that has appeared on the scene:

"The function of God has been changed. He has a whole new role. No longer is he the object of all worship and adoration. Instead he has become an important means for getting what we now worship and adore—things, or at least the money to buy the things.

In our brave new world we worship the things we have been conditioned to want, and we will be religious if religion can guarantee us the products our democratic capitalistic society turns out by the tons."

This "new Jesus" propagates a 'prosperity theology' that promises the faithful if they seek first the kingdom of this reconstructed deity and do all the things the pop religious books say will guarantee success, then all these things (the ones described in the ads) will be added unto them. This is a new religion that is functional, fit for these new believers who hunger for consumer goods. It has, as they say, 'user-friendly churches' that are just right for people who will help us succeed in life…which of course means to get all the things we don't need, so as to gratify our media-created hungers.

From time to time, a person comes along and reminds us of the other Jesus. We admire her and him, but then we hurry back to that "new" Jesus who doesn't demand sacrifices for the poor and oppressed but simply promises to be there to help us. The ad for the army suggests, All That WE Can Be.

- What has the Word of Faith Movement done with the concept of God?

Answer: They have turned God into a mere _____ that supposedly can be tapped into by faith to satisfy our lust for _____

_____ .

God, through the Apostle Peter's pen, warned us about this kind of monetary manipulation in the church in the last days:

2 Peter 2:1-3 states: "But there were also false prophets in Israel, just as there will be false teachers among you. _____ _____

_____ they will make up clever lies to _____

_____ _____ _____ _____.

But God condemned them long ago, and their destruction is on the way."

THE 2ND REASON SO MANY PEOPLE HAVE ABANDONED THE CHRISTIAN FAITH - A FOCUS ON MAKING _____

_____ _____; **(OR IN**

OTHER   WORDS)   THE   _____

_____ MOVEMENT.

- Through this movement, how are many people in the Church led astray?

Answer: By _____ manipulation.

- What do the leaders of this movement claim that true and loving Christians will have?

Answer: An _____ mind when it comes to understanding the Bible. They say that _____ not _____, provide the foundation for Christianity. In other words, your version of Christianity is what feels right for you.

- So in essence, what does the person do?
Answer: You make up _____ _____ doctrine.

- What doctrines, right now, are main-line denominations battling over?
Answer:

✓ Whether or not Jesus really is the _____ way to heaven.

✓ Many people claiming to be Christians are actually _____ the existence of hell.

✓ _____ of homosexuality as a _____ lifestyle; now saying, "It's _____ even for those behind the pulpit."

People are _____ doctrine to suit their own _____ fancies.

To show the proof of this, Pastor Billy shares some samples of perverting the actual text of the Bible to make up their own version of the Bible:

The Politically Correct Version

Since many readers today find the Bible sexist, racist, elitist and insensitive, the Oxford University Press released a culturally sensitive version of the Bible. "In this version God is no longer ' _____ ' and Jesus is no longer

' _____ '.

- In the majestic opening of John's Gospel, 'the glory he has from the Father as the only Son of the Father' becomes 'the glory as of a _____ only _____.' (John 1:14)

- The Lord's prayer now begins like this: 'Father-_____, hallowed be your name. May your dominion come.' (Luke 11:2)

- Jesus' own self-understanding as God's only son is generalized to: 'No one knows the _____ except the Father-_____; and no one knows the Father-_____ except the _____...' (Matthew 11:27)

- Avoiding another traditional phrase, 'Son of Man,' the Oxford text reads: 'Then they will see 'the _____ one in clouds with great power and glory.' (Mark 13:26)

The New Feminist Version

A new edition of the Gospels identifies Christ as a woman named

"_____ Christ" of Nazareth. The LBI Institute wanted to

_____ the _____ of Christ and God. Billie

Shakespeare, the vice president for the publisher, stated the following:

"This long-awaited revised text of the Gospels makes the moral message of

Christ more _____ to many, and more _____ to

all." He also said, "It is _____. We published this new Bible to

acknowledge the rise of _____ in society."

In this feminist version:

✓ the Prodigal _____becomes the Prodigal _____ .

✓ the _____ prayer becomes the _____ prayer.

- In Luke chapter 2 the verses now read, "And Joseph went to
  Bethlehem. To be enrolled with Mary, his wife, who was then
  pregnant. And she brought forth her firstborn child. And
  _____ name was chosen to be _____ ."

- A passage on the crucifixion, from John 19 says, 'And _____
  bearing _____ cross went forth. There they crucified
  _____ .'

- And a resurrection passage from Matthew 28 now states, 'Mary Magdalene and the other Mary came to see the tomb. But the angel said to the women, 'Do not be afraid, for I know that you come to see _____ who was crucified. _____ is not here; for _____ is risen."

The New Postmodern Version

This new version has an evolutionary slant to the gospel and presents Jesus as being born, 'not to a virgin, but to a _____ .'

The first volume in the series "mixes the best of each wisdom tradition with the latest findings in psychology, quantum physics, neuroscience, and linguistics." When covering the Gospel of Mark it includes these 3 parables:

- ✓ The Parable of the _____ .
- ✓ The Parable of the _____ _____ .
- ✓ The Parable of the _____ .

In a quote from the Parable of the Gorilla, the writer states, "Yes, if Jesus was alive today, he would understand that his ancestors, just like ours, were _____. No, he wouldn't run around claiming he was born of a virgin."

•   What has a Postmodern, Liberal society done with Biblical terminology?

Answer: They have _____ it.

Note some examples:

What our Founding Fathers referred to as 'drunkenness' because of their Christian heritage, we now call _____ and deem it a social disease, rather than a sin.

What the Law of God called 'sodomy'; we now call an _____ life style, giving this a political identity and the unassuming name of gay rights and sexual orientation. Pornography is a perversion that brings death to a nation, and yet we call it _____ _____.

What our Founding Fathers called "immorality", we now call it the _____ _____; what the law called "adultery" or "fornication", we now call _____ _____ or _____ _____; and what the Law called "abhorrent social behavior" (stealing or filthy language), we now call _____ social _____ or "anti-social behavior."

In these last days, people "in the Church are deliberately, gathering around themselves liberal teachers, to tell them _____ they want to hear, while _____ the Truth-just like Paul said would happen:

2 Timothy 4:3-4 states: "For a time is coming when people will no longer listen to right teaching. They will follow their own desires and will look for teachers who will tell them whatever they want to hear. They will reject the truth and follow strange myths."

Yes, in these last days before Jesus comes again, people will _____ to be Christians, yet will also, _____ follow _____ teachers. The

Bible clearly tells us that "these "religious" people are sadly in-line for the ultimate rude awakening from Jesus Himself."

Matthew 7:7-21-23 states, "Not all people who sound religious are really godly. They may refer to me as 'Lord,' but they still won't enter the Kingdom of Heaven. The decisive issue is whether they obey my Father in Heaven."

On judgment day many will tell me, 'Lord, Lord, we prophesied in your name and cast out demons in your name and performed many miracles in your name.' But I will reply, 'I never knew you. Go away; the things you did were unauthorized."

My friends, Christ's 2nd Coming is rapidly approaching. Are you ready to meet Jesus? The Rise of Apostasy is another vivid proof of His soon return.

In Luke 21:28, Jesus declared, "When these things begin to take place, stand up and lift up your heads, because your redemption is drawing near."

Chapter Seven

One World Religion

Hey, how many of you have learned this lesson in life yet: the longer you live, rather than finding all the answers to all of life's problems, you actually discover that the questions about life seem to get even more weird? Anybody notice besides me? Well, for those of you who didn't raise your hands, that's right, I'm here to help you out. You see, I've been keeping a list of some of the weird questions that I've come across in this life. Let's see if they sound familiar to you:

1. Would a chicken crossing the road be considered poultry in motion?
2. Isn't it true that he who dies with the most toys, is still dead?
3. Is the reason why a chicken coop has two doors is because if it had four, it would be a chicken sedan?
4. Who was the first person to look at a cow and say, "I think I'll squeeze these dangly things here, and drink whatever comes out"?
5. Why do toasters always have a setting that burns the toast to a horrible crisp in which no decent human being would ever eat?
6. If Jimmy cracks corn and no one cares, why is there a song about him?
7. Can a hearse carrying a corpse drive in the carpool lane?
8. If Wile E. Coyote had enough money to buy all that Acme stuff, why didn't he just buy dinner?

9. Isn't it true that there is always a reason to smile because every 7 minutes of every day, someone in an aerobics class is pulling a hamstring?
10. Isn't it true that when your mother asks, "Do you want a piece of advice?" it's a mere formality. Because it doesn't matter if you answer yes or no. You're still going to get it anyway?[1]

Now, as you guys can see, there are some pretty weird questions to try to figure out in life, aren't there? But to me, I think the weirdest thing that I question in life would have to be this: how is it that people can hear the good news that God will freely forgive them of all their sins through Jesus and save them from the wrath to come, and yet just turn and walk away. Now folks, that's not only weird, it's unfortunate. Because this means that they are sadly running the risk of being left behind and will be catapulted into the seven-year Tribulation that is coming upon the whole world.

And folks, the time of the Tribulation is not a party. Jesus said in **Matthew 24** that it would be a time of greater horror than anything the world has ever seen or will ever see again. He also said that unless that time of calamity is shortened, the entire human race would be destroyed. But God is not only a God of wrath; He's a God of love as well. And **because He loves you and I**, He has given us many warning signs so that we would know when the Tribulation could be near and that Christ's 2nd Coming is rapidly approaching. Therefore, to make sure our lives aren't filled with even more weird questions from being left behind, we're going to continue taking a look at **The Final Countdown**.

We already saw how the **#10** sign on **The Final Countdown** was **The Jewish People**. The **#9** sign was **Modern Technology**. The **#8** sign was **Worldwide Upheaval**. The **#7** sign was **The Rise of Falsehood**. The **#6** sign was **The Rise of Wickedness**. And in the last chapter we saw how the **#5** sign was none other than **The Rise of Apostasy**. There we saw that God lovingly foretold you and I that when we see an increase of people in the Church turning away from the truth, that this would be an indicator that we are in the last days. Isn't that what we see **today** through the Church Growth Movement, Word of Faith Movement, The Signs and Wonders Movement, and Liberal Christianity?

But that's not the only signs that God has given us. The **#4** sign on **The Final Countdown** is none other than **A One World Religion**. So just what are these specific prophesies being fulfilled today concerning **A One World Religion**, revealing that we could be in the last days? Well, I'm glad you asked. Let's take a look. The **1ˢᵗ End Time Prophecy** concerning **A One World Religion** is that **there will be a worldwide worship of the antichrist**.

Revelation 13:3,4,8 "The whole world was astonished and followed the beast. Men worshiped the dragon because he had given authority to the beast, and they also worshiped the beast and asked, 'Who is like the beast? Who can make war against him?' All inhabitants of the earth will worship the beast – all whose names have not been written in the book of life belonging to the Lamb that was slain from the creation of the world." (NIV)

According to this passage of Scripture, there is coming a day when all the inhabitants of the earth will be busy worshipping the antichrist himself, who, as other passages state, will actually declare himself to be a god and demand worship. One day, the whole world will literally be unified into **A One World Religion** that is actually **satanically inspired**. But the question is, "Could that really happen? Could the whole world really be deceived into creating **A One World Religion**? And is there any evidence that this is really going to take place just like the Bible said?" You bet there is! Let's take a look.

The **1ˢᵗ way** we know that we are headed for **A One World Religion** is due to a **Watering Down of the Truth**. That's right, I'm talking about the **Ecumenical Movement**. You see if you're going to deceive people into creating

A One World Religion then you must certainly get rid of any sense of absolute rights or wrongs. And this is precisely what the Ecumenical movement is doing.

For those of you who may not know, Ecumenicalism is defined as "the organized attempt to bring about the cooperation and unity of all believers in Christ."[2] Now, on the surface this sounds really good, doesn't it? Except what they don't tell you is that unity is being sought not on the basis of truth, but from a watered down version of it. For instance, they say that, for the sake of the gospel, you and I need to now get along with and join hands with anyone and everyone who claims to be a Christian and names the Name of Christ. But the problem is that many of the cults claim to be Christians and name the Name of Christ, but that doesn't mean they're true believers does it? Do you see the danger in all of this?

You see, instead of broadening the gospel, people are now compromising the truth and redefining what it means to be a Christian. And now, those who take a stand for sound teaching and correct doctrine are being labeled as "divisive" and "unloving." But the funny thing is that Jesus Himself said that it is exclusively His truth that sets us free, not a watered down version of it. Besides you cannot have true unity in the Body of Christ without understanding what truth is. Furthermore, we are told in the Bible to diligently keep ourselves pure from apostasy and heresy, not to embrace it. We are told to discern and watch out for false gospels, not to accept them under the guise of working together. Besides, truth by its very nature is divisive. It is the only way in which we can **divide** between what is right and wrong. Watering down the truth for supposed unity is not true unity. What this actually does is lead, not only to a false gospel, but also to a false idea of who God is. This is precisely what has happened today.

"Salad-bar religion denotes the trend where people pick and choose religious beliefs, doctrines and practices – mixing and matching them much as they would select food in a cafeteria.

This is not just popular among non-Christians, but also among people who consider themselves to be Christians. People borrow from different traditions, then add them to whatever religion they're used to. But they don't want anything to do with organized religion.

Americans write their own Bible. They fashion their own God. More often than not, the God they choose is more like a best friend who has endless time for their needs, no matter how trivial.

Scholars call this, 'domesticating God,' turning Him into a social planner, therapist, or guardian angel. We have trivialized God. We assume that God is the butler who serves you for one reason, to give you a happy life. We've turned Him into a divine Prozac."[3]

People, if we keep compromising the truth just for the sake of "getting along" with all who name the name of Christ, we will not only continue to come up with a different version of God, but a different gospel as well. Besides, truth will always offend those who don't want to hear it! And if you really love somebody, you will love them enough to tell the truth of the gospel even if it hurts, because of the horrible consequences, namely hell. Truth is serious business. One thing you don't want to get wrong is where you're going to spend eternity. And what the ecumenical movement has done, under the guise of "unity" and supposed "love," is to embrace all forms of heresy and even a false gospel. This means that people could actually be fooled into thinking that they are on their way to heaven, when in reality, they're going to hell! Now, is that loving? I don't think so!

Besides, you tell me, can we really "get along" with those who are claiming to be Christians yet state that one has to keep the sacraments to be saved, or that satan doesn't exist, or that hell is only make believe? Can we really "join hands" with those who would have you and I believe that Jesus isn't God but actually the archangel Michael, or worse yet, that He is the spirit-brother of lucifer? I think the answer is obvious, especially when the Bible deliberately says to not only **stay away from them** but to certainly not cooperate with them in propagating heresy!

Romans 16:17-18 "I urge you, brothers, to watch out for those who cause divisions and put obstacles in your way that are contrary to the teaching you have learned. Keep away from them. For such people are not serving our Lord Christ, but their own appetites. By smooth talk and flattery they deceive the minds of naive people." (NIV)

As you can see, rather than creating unity, these false teachers of Ecumenicalism and their false teachings are actually the one's who are causing division! Hmmm. You mean there would actually come a time when people would team up with false teachers who use smooth talk to deceive people into accepting a watered down version of the truth where everybody is right and nobody is wrong, making it easy to go along with **A One World Religion**? That would be, **uh huh**. So is it any wonder that there's been so many people falling for this push for **A One World Religion**, just like the Bible said? When? In the last days.

The **2nd way** we know that we are headed for **A One World Religion** is because of a **Worldwide Assault on Christians**. That's right, I'm talking about **Christian Persecution**. You see, if you're going to deceive people into creating **A One World Religion** then you must certainly get rid of those who are standing in the way. And can you guess just who that might be? And this is precisely why Christian persecution has skyrocketed in recent years. And how ironic it is that everybody knows that Hitler killed 6 millions Jews, right? But how many realize that he murdered 7 million Christians?[4] Oh, but that's not all. **Right now**, there are over 200 million Christians worldwide under the threat of persecution.[5] **Right now**, all over the world, fellow brothers and sisters in Christ are being beaten, tortured, imprisoned, and murdered. Why? Because they refuse to compromise the truth, unlike the ecumenical movement. In 1988 alone some 310,000 Christians were slaughtered.[6] In fact, more Christians have died for their faith in this century alone than in the previous nineteen centuries combined.[7]

Now, I don't know about you guys, but it sure looks to me like somebody is desperately trying to get rid of those who are standing in the way. What do you think? But that's not the half of it. People are projecting that it's only a matter of time before we see this kind of open persecution of Christians right here in America. What? Persecution in America? Could that really happen? Folks, it not only can happen, it has already begun! Let's take a look at **just a few** examples.

1. In recent decades, the Bible, prayer, and Ten Commandments were taken out of the schools.
2. Lawyers are asking that the Bible be placed on the list of books considered dangerous for children.
3. The sharing of the gospel is now being equated as a form of "mental manipulation."
4. The media consistently portrays those who believe in the Bible as cultists and stereotype Christians as being ignorant, homophobic, greedy, hypocritical, and sexually deviant.
5. The U.S. Supreme Court judges ordered the end of school sponsored religious activities, such as prayers during morning announcements.
6. Tourists visiting Washington D.C. were ordered by police to stop praying in the rotunda of the U.S. Capitol.
7. The ACLU put pressure on a town to remove the fish symbol from its official logo calling it a "secret sign of Christianity."
8. A minister was arrested for praying on the steps of the Supreme Court.
9. Requests have been made to do away with the Pledge of Allegiance because of its mention of God.

10. Hate Crime bills are now being considered that would completely silence pulpits across America and imprison Pastors as well as any Christian who violates them.[8]

I'd say the heat is being turned up, how about you? One person stated, "It is illegal in U.S. public schools to read the Bible, but many states require that a Bible is provided for every convict in jail. So if the children can't read the Bible in school, they'll be able to read it when they get to prison."[9]

Now, as incredible as this may sound, it's even crazier to listen to the justification as to why it has been declared to be open hunting season on us Christians. For instance, they say that we are being **judgmental** because we say that they are not good enough for God. But the Bible says that "no one is righteous, no not one." (Romans 3) They say that we are being **arrogant** because we think we've found the only way to eternal life. But Jesus said, "He is the way, the truth, and the life, and that nobody comes to the Father except through Him." (John 14:6) They say that we are being **narrow-minded** because if we practiced what we preach, we would see all people worthy of salvation. But the Bible says that "no one is worthy, no not one." (Romans 3) They say that we are being **ignorant** because we ignore other paths to enlightenment. But Jesus said he was the ultimate Truth not one of many. (John 14:6) They say that we are being **old-fashioned** because we cling to obsolete myths. But the Bible says that it is the truth we are to cling to even when the whole world is turning aside to myths. (2 Timothy 4)[10]

And just to make sure that we sound really bad in the public arena, we are now being labeled with such terms as, "psycho groups," "harmful and dangerous sects," "obstructionist right-wing fanatics who embrace a message of hate and fear (quote from Bill Clinton)," "mongers of hate who preach their anger (quote from Texas Governor Ann Richards)," "intolerant, using subterranean tactics (quote from Congressman Vic Fazio)," "unchristian religious right who are selling our children out in the name of religion (quote from U.S. Surgeon General Joycelyn Elders)," "a greater threat than the old threat of communism (New York Times writer)," "fire-breathing radicals," "merchants of hate," "fanatics," and even "militants and bigots," and even "right wing fundamental extremists."[11] Hey, wait a second. That's the same terminology they're using for the Muslim terrorists who everyone says we need to get rid of? People you better wake up! They're already using the same propaganda on us and so that means we're next! Don't believe me? Check out this quote from Janet Reno who gives us her **definition of a cultist**:

"A cultist is one who has a strong belief in the Bible and the Second Coming of Christ; who frequently attends Bible studies; who has a high level of financial giving to a Christian cause; who home schools their children; who has accumulated survival foods and has a strong belief in the Second Amendment; and who distrusts big government.

Any of these may qualify [a person as a cultist] but certainly more than one [of these] would cause us to look at this person as a threat, and his family as being in a risk situation that qualified for government interference."[12]

Now, does anybody besides me come to the obvious conclusion that **we are in a serious spiritual battle right here in America**? But if these facts about the rise of persecution have caught you off guard, it really shouldn't have. Why? Because Jesus made it clear that this kind of hatred towards the Church is to be expected. When? In the last days!

Matthew 24:9 "Then you will be arrested, persecuted, and killed. You will be hated all over the world because of your allegiance to me." (NLT)

Hmmm. You mean there's actually coming a time when Christians will be slandered and slaughtered worldwide just because they follow Jesus and refuse to go along with **A One World Religion**? That would be, **uh huh**. So is it any wonder that there's been so many people falling for this push for **A One World Religion**, just like the Bible said? When? In the last days.

The **3ʳᵈ way** we know that we are headed for **A One World Religion** is because of a **Welcoming of All Faiths**. That's right, I'm talking about the **Interfaithism Movement**. You see, if you're going to deceive people into creating **A One World Religion** then you must certainly get rid of any sense of one religion being superior over the other. And this is precisely what the Interfaithism Movement has done. Promoters of this movement would have you and I believe that all religions are valid pathways to God. Therefore, there's no need to argue or fight with one another. We just need to respect, tolerate and find common ground with one another. We need to work together for the common cause of saving the earth and keeping humanity from destroying itself. Hmmm. Kind of sounds like the ecumenical movement, doesn't it? After all, especially in light of the terrorist attacks on September 11ᵗʰ, are we not being told that "religious differences" are the main cause of war?

But once again, this is compromising the truth for the sake of a false sense of unity. The term interfaithism might sound nice, but as far as the Bible is concerned, there is no such thing. An interfaith Christian is an oxymoron. Besides, according to their own definition, Jesus was apparently the most intolerant person who ever lived because he clearly stated that,

John 14:6 "I am the way and the truth and the life. No one comes to the Father except through me." (NIV)

Now, I don't know about you guys, but that is one of the most "intolerant" statements a person could make in today's world. But remember, Jesus, Who is God, is the one who said it! Is anyone really prepared to call Him intolerant or even a bigot? I don't think so! And besides, can we really "get along" with those who believe that the world was created by the blood of an elephant, or that we will burn in a mythical limbo place to purge away our sins before we can go to heaven, or that we ourselves are gods? Can we really "join hands" with those who would have you and I believe that sin and evil is just an illusion, or that hell is only make believe and that heaven for some men will be to endlessly satisfy their lust with as many virgins as they want? I think the answer is obvious, especially when the Bible deliberately says to **come out and be separate from them**!

2 Corinthians 6:14-17 "Don't team up with those who are unbelievers. How can goodness be a partner with wickedness? How can light live with darkness? What harmony can there be between Christ and the Devil? How can a believer be a partner with an unbeliever?

And what union can there be between God's temple and idols? For we are the temple of the living God. As God said: 'I will live in them and walk among them. I will be their God, and they will be my people. Therefore, come out from them and separate yourselves from them, says the Lord.'" (NLT)

Now, you might be tempted to think that there's no way that people are going to be able to pull off this Interfaithism Movement and create **A One World Religion**. Nobody is ever going to fall for this. But what most people don't realize is that it's not only **going to be** put into place but it's already well on it's way to becoming the **New World Religion**, and has even been in the planning stages for a long time. Here, see the progress for yourself:

1. 1893: 1st World Parliament of Religions held
2. 1930: World Congress of Faiths
3. 1948: World Council of Churches
4. 1970: World Conference of Religions for Peace Started
5. 1974: 2nd World Conference of Religions for Peace
6. 1979: 3rd World Conference of Religions for Peace
7. 1984: 4th World Conference of Religions for Peace

8. 1986: Vatican calls for a meeting of all religions to come and pray for world peace
9. 1989: 5th World Conference of Religions for Peace
10. 1993: 2nd World Parliament of Religions held with largest gathering of religious leaders in history
11. 1993: The Declaration of Global Ethic – A new set of commandments for the world
12. 1994: 6th World Conference of Religions for Peace
13. 1997: Charter written for the United Religions Organization
14. 1999: 7th World Conference of Religions for Peace
15. 2000: United Religions Organization charter signed by most of the world's religions
16. 2000: World Peace Summit of Religious and Spiritual Leaders – signing of Commitment to Global Peace and creation of World Council of Religions
17. 2001: World Congress on the Preservation of Religious Diversity
18. 2002: Vatican calls for a meeting of all religions to come and pray for peace and to overcome conflict
19. 2002: 1st meeting of World Council of Religions
20. 2002: World Conference of Women Religious and Spiritual Leaders
21. 2002: World Peace Summit Established by World Conference of Religions for Peace
22. 2003: 2nd World Peace Summit
23. 2003: Pope commends peace of world to Mary
24. 2003: Pope urges unity against violence among World Religions
25. 2003: Inter-religious tribute given on behalf of Mother Teresa
26. 2004: 3rd World Peace Summit
27. 2004: Vatican hosts Interfaith Concert
28. 2004: Pope says religions must unite for peace
29. 2005: 4th World Peace Summit
30. 2005: World Council of Churches asks Pope for renewed commitment to ecumenicalism
31. 2005: Global Day of Prayer unites diverse Churches
32. 2005: Vatican promotes Unity at World Mission Conference
33. 2006: 8th World Conference of Religions for Peace
34. 2006: Pope encourages more Inter-Religious prayer meetings
35. 2006: 5th World Peace Summit
36. 2006: World Religions unite over Global Warming
37. 2006: 2nd Global Day of Prayer

38. 2006: Pope and Dalai Lama herald peace between Catholics, Buddhists, and Hindus
39. 2006: Pope's praying in a Mosque deemed a "New Horizon" in Interfaith
40. 2007: 6th World Peace Summit
41. 2007: Interfaith Council established for Jerusalem
42. 2007: 3rd Global Day of Prayer
43. 2007:Groups in U.S. declare that all paths lead to God
44. 2007: World Council of Churches encourages different religions to unify in diversity
45. 2008: 7th World Peace Summit
46. 2008: World Council of Churches and Pope seek cooperation
47. 2008: Pope meets with Jewish, Islamic, Buddhist, Jain, Hindu leaders in Washington
48. 2008: 4th Global Day of Prayer[13]

Now, how many of you have heard about this on the news lately? Of course not! And as if that wasn't eye opening enough, in light of this information, it now makes sense why we see people, like media mogul Ted Turner of CNN, paying for most of the costs of the World Peace Summit of Religious Leaders and making comments like this, "What disturbed me is that my religious Christian sect was very intolerant. We thought we were the only ones going to heaven."[14] Hmmm. I wonder if he's hoping to create GNN, the Global News Network? And now it makes sense as to why Prince Charles of England launched a new movement called Respect, in order to promote tolerance among the world's religions.[15] Now I can see why people like Al Gore are making statements like this:

"The richness and diversity of our religious tradition throughout history is a spiritual resource long ignored by people of faith, who are often afraid to open their minds to teachings first offered outside their own system of belief. But the emergence of a civilization in which knowledge moves freely and almost instantaneously through the world has...spurred a renewed investigation of the wisdom distilled by all faiths. This panreligious perspective may prove especially important where our global civilization's responsibility for the earth is concerned."[16]

Now, I would say that somebody is taking this **One World Religion** very seriously, how about you? But they're not the only ones. So is the occult. In fact, the New Age occult, which is behind this whole thing, has their own idea of how this creation of **A One World Religion** is going to come about.[17] What's interesting is how it sounds strikingly similar to what the Bible says is going to take place. For instance, they believe that once all the world's religions come together, (and they're expecting it soon) a religious leader will be chosen to be earth's religious spokesman and will then encourage all the people of the world to accept a new world leader, who will suddenly appear on the scene. Hmmm. Kind of sounds like the false prophet the Bible talks about, who convinces the world to worship the Beast or the antichrist, doesn't it?

Revelation 13:11-15 "Then I saw another beast come up out of the earth. He had two horns like those of a lamb, and he spoke with the voice of a dragon. He exercised all the authority of the first beast. And he required all the earth and those who belong to this world to worship the first beast, whose death-wound had been healed. He did astounding miracles, such as making fire flash down to earth from heaven while everyone was watching.

And with all the miracles he was allowed to perform on behalf of the first beast, he deceived all the people who belong to this world. He ordered the people of the world to make a great statue of the first beast, who was fatally wounded and then came back to life. He was permitted to give life to this statue so that it could speak. Then the statue commanded that anyone refusing to worship it must die." (NLT)

Oh, but that's not all. What's really interesting is how the occult is in agreement that none of this can fully take place until the people who will never go along with this **One World Religion** are out of the way. Can you guess who that might be? In fact, strangely enough, they say that these people that are restraining or holding things up **won't necessarily die** but will somehow mysteriously disappear, or in their words, "**elect to leave this dimension as if going to another room**." And once these people leave this earth, the occult says the new world leader will take his rightful place over the world. Hmmm. Kind of sounds like the rapture of the Church again doesn't it, and how once the restraining presence of the Holy Spirit through the Church is gone, that this is precisely when the antichrist will appear.

2 Thessalonians 2:7-8 "For the mystery of lawlessness is already at work; only he who now restrains will do so until he is taken out of the way. Then that lawless one will be revealed whom the Lord will slay with the breath of His mouth and bring to an end by the appearance of His coming." (NAS)

Hmmm. You mean there would actually come a time when people all over the earth will be waiting for the Church to disappear so they can then be unified in **A One World Religion**? Could that really happen? People, it's already happening before our very eyes. When? In the last days.

And believe it or not, even with all this amazing evidence pointing to the signs of Christ's soon return, some people are still living with a false sense of security by thinking that things will never get worse than they already are, like this guy:

"One day a man was having a pleasant day driving down the road when a police officer pulled him over. However, instead of a giving him a ticket, the officer informed him that, because he was wearing his seat belt, he had just won $5,000 in a safety competition. The man couldn't believe it! His day was getting better by the minute.

So the officer asked, "What are you going to do with the prize money?"

But the man responded before thinking about who it was he was talking to and blurted out, 'I guess I'll go to driving school and get my license.'

And just when things couldn't have gotten worse, the man's wife, who was seated next to him, chimed in, 'Officer, don't listen to him. He's always a smart aleck when he's drunk.'

Then as if that wasn't bad enough, this woke up the guy in the back seat, who, when he saw the cop, blurted out, 'I knew we wouldn't get far in this stolen car.'

And believe it or not, at that moment, there was a knock from the trunk and a voice asked 'Are we over the border yet?'"[18]

Now, that guy found out real fast that life can change dramatically for the worse in just a short amount of time, didn't he? But believe it or not, did you know that he's not alone? You see, many people today think that their lives are going to always remain the same and even get better through **A One World Religion**. They will even cry out that we are entering an era of unprecedented peace and safety. However, the Bible warns that this false security in a false religion will quickly turn into utter destruction by the coming of the Lord Jesus Himself.

1 Thessalonians 5:1-3 "But as to the suitable times and the precise seasons and dates, brethren, you have no necessity for anything being written to you. For you yourselves know perfectly well that the day of the [return of the] Lord will come [as unexpectedly and suddenly] as a thief in the night.

When people are saying, All is well and secure, and, There is peace and safety, then in a moment unforeseen destruction (ruin and death) will come upon them as suddenly as labor pains come upon a woman with child; and they shall by no means escape, for there will be no escape." (AMP)

People of God, I hope you're not one of those who have bought into this lie that man can somehow spawn his own utopia by creating **A One World Religion**. Why? Because you might wake up one day and discover that **you've been left behind**. And do you know what? God doesn't want you left behind. Because He loves you and I, He has given us the warning sign of **A One World**

Religion to show us that the Tribulation **could be near** and that Christ's 2nd Coming is rapidly approaching. Jesus Himself said this:

Luke 21:28 "When these things begin to take place, stand up and lift up your heads, because your redemption is drawing near." (NIV)

Like it or not folks, we are headed for **The Final Countdown**. We don't know the day or the hour. Only God knows. The point is, if you're a Christian, it's time to stop living for yourself and start living for our Savior! Folks, it's high time we Christians speak up and declare the good news of salvation to those who are dying all around us. But please, if you're not a Christian, give your life to Jesus today, because tomorrow may be too late! Just like the Bible said!

Study Questions

Review

Let's do things a little different this time. By drawing a line try matching up the sermon title with the number of the sign.

The Rise of Wickedness	**Sign #10**
The Rise of Apostasy	**Sign #9**
The Jewish People	**Sign #8**
Worldwide Upheaval	**Sign #7**
The Rise of Falsehood	**Sign #6**
Modern Technology	**Sign #5**

This Chapter:

The #4 sign on the Final Countdown is none other than a _____

_____ _____. The Bible tells us in Revelation

13:3, 4, 8 that there will come in the last days a _____ worship of the

_____.

Revelation 13:3,4,8 "The whole world was astonished and followed the beast. Men worshiped the dragon because he had given authority to the beast, and they also worshiped the beast and asked, 'Who is like the beast? Who can make war against him?' All inhabitants of the earth will worship the beast – all whose names have not been written in the book of life belonging to the Lamb that was slain from the creation of the world."

> ## "ONE DAY, THE WHOLE WORLD WILL LITERALLY BE UNIFIED INTO A ONE WORLD RELIGION THAT IS ACTUALLY _____ INSPIRED."

- Is there any evidence today that our world is headed in this direction?

Answer: Yes! and Pastor Billy is about to share with us three evidences of this.

THE 1ST EVIDENCE

The first evidence that we know that we are headed for a One World Religion is a _____ down of the _____; or to put it in other terms, the _____ Movement.

- If you're going to deceive people into creating a One World Religion, what must you get rid of?

Answer: Any sense of _____ rights or wrongs.

In the Ecumenical Movement unity is being sought, _____ on the basis _____, but from a _____ _____ version of it.

For example, they will say today that, for the sake of the gospel, "you and I need to now get along with and join hands with _____ and

_____ who _____ to be a Christian and names the Name of Christ."

- What is the big problem with that concept?

Answer: Many of the _____ claim to be Christians.

In this worldwide movement people are now _____ the truth and _____ what it means to be a Christian.

- How do those, with this 'ecumenicalism' mindset, view others who take a stand for sound teaching and correct doctrine?

Answer: We are labeled as '_____' and '_____'.

I guess Jesus Himself would have also been given such a label by these people.

- What did Jesus say it is that sets a person free?

Answer: Exclusively _____ truth…not a watered down version of it.

- What else did Pastor Billy share?
Answer:
  ✓ You cannot have _____ unity in the Body of Christ without understanding what truth is.

✓ We are told in the Bible to diligently keep ourselves pure from

_____ and _____, not to _____ it.

✓ We are told to _____ and watch out for _____
gospels, not to accept them under the guise of working together.

✓ Truth by its very nature is _____. It is the only way in
which we can _____ between what is right and wrong.
Watering down the truth for supposed unity is _____ true unity.

• What does "Salad-bar religion" denote? Here are some examples:
  ✓ People pick and choose religious beliefs, doctrines and practices
    – mixing and matching them much as they would select food in a
    cafeteria.

  Put down as many thoughts as you can:

_____
_____
_____
_____

Pastor Billy shared, truth is _____ business.

• What is one truth that you don't want to get wrong?

Answer: _____ you're going to spend _____.

People could actually be fooled into thinking that they are on their way to

_____, when in reality, they're going to _____!

All under the guise of "unity" and supposed "love".

How can true Christians really "get along" with people who hold to the following beliefs?

    ✓ One has to keep the sacraments to be saved.
    ✓ Satan doesn't even exist.
    ✓ Hell is only make believe.
    ✓ Jesus isn't God, but actually the archangel Michael.
    ✓ Jesus is the spirit-brother of Lucifer.

Romans 16:17-18 tells us to stay away from people who believe such things; never to cooperate with them. "I urge you, brothers, to watch out for those who cause divisions and put obstacles in your way that are contrary to the teaching you have learned. Keep away from them. For such people are not serving our Lord Christ, but their own appetites. By smooth talk and flattery they deceive the minds of naive people."

THE 2ND EVIDENCE

The second evidence that we know that we are headed for a One World Religion

is _____ _____ on Christians; or to put it in other

terms, Christian _____ .

•   How many Christians today worldwide, are under the threat of

       persecution?

Answer: Over 200 _____.

•   Why are our fellow brothers and sisters in Christ being beaten, tortured,

       imprisoned and murdered?

Answer: Because they refuse to _____ the truth.

- Could this kind of open persecution of Christians ever happen in America?

Answer: It has already begun!

1. In recent decades, the Bible, prayer, and Ten Commandments were taken out of the schools.

2. Lawyers are asking that the Bible be placed on the list of books considered dangerous for children.

3. The sharing of the gospel is now being equated as a form of "mental manipulation."

4. The media consistently portrays those who believe in the Bible as cultists and stereotype Christians as being ignorant, homophobic, greedy, hypocritical, and sexually deviant.

5. The U.S. Supreme Court judges ordered the end of school sponsored religious activities, such as prayers during morning announcements.

6. Tourists visiting Washington D.C. were ordered by police to stop praying in the rotunda of the U.S. Capitol.

7. The ACLU put pressure on a town to remove the fish symbol from its official logo calling it a "secret sign of Christianity."

8. A minister was arrested for praying on the steps of the Supreme Court.

9. Requests have been made to do away with the Pledge of Allegiance because of its mention of God.

10. Hate Crime bills are now being considered that would completely silence pulpits across America and imprison Pastors as well as any Christian who violates them.

Pastor Billy called the assault on Christians as "open hunting season".

- What do these people say about us?

Answer:
  - ✓ They say, that we are being _____ because we say that they are not good enough for God.

Yet the Bible declares in Romans 3:10, "no one is righteous, no not one".

  - ✓ They say, that we are being _____ because we think we've found the only way to eternal life.

Yet Jesus said in John 14:6, "I am the way, the truth, and the life; no one comes to the Father except through Me."

  - ✓ They say, that we are being _____-_____ because if we practiced what we preached, we would see all people worthy of salvation.

But the Bible says that, "no one is worthy, no not one" in Romans 3.

  - ✓ They say, that we are being _____ because we ignore other paths to enlightenment.

But Jesus said that, "He was the ultimate Truth, not one of many in John chapter 14 verse 6.

  - ✓ They say that we are being _____-_____ because we cling to obsolete myths.

But the Bible says that it is the truth we are to cling to even when the whole world turns aside to myths in 2 Timothy 4:3-4.

- What are some of the labels being given to Christians in the public arena?

Answer:
- ✓ _____ groups
- ✓ Harmful and _____ sects
- ✓ "_____ right-wing fanatics who embrace a message of _____ and fear" (quote by Bill Clinton).
- ✓ "Mongers of hate who preached their anger" (Governor Ann Richards)
- ✓ "Intolerant, using subterranean tactics" (Congressman Vic Fazio)
- ✓ "A greater threat than the old threat of Communism" (New York times writer)
- ✓ "_____ religious right who are selling our children out in the name of religion" (U.S. Surgeon General, Joycelyn Elders)
- ✓ "Fire-breathing radicals"
- ✓ "Merchants of _____ "
- ✓ "Fanatics"
- ✓ "Militants and _____ "
- ✓ "Right-wing fundamental _____ "

Note this quote from Janet Reno on her definition of a cultist:

"A cultist is one who has a strong belief in the Bible and the Second Coming of Christ; who frequently attends Bible studies; who has a high level of financial giving to a Christian cause; who home schools their children; who has accumulated survival foods and has a strong belief in the Second Amendment; and who distrusts big government.

Any of these may qualify [a person as a cultist] but certainly more than one [of these] would cause us to look at this person as a threat, and his family as being in a risk situation that qualified for government interference."

Jesus told us in Matthew 24:9 that this kind of hatred towards the church was to be expected, "Then you will be arrested, persecuted, and killed. You will be hated all over the world because of your allegiance to me."

THE 3RD EVIDENCE

The third evidence that we know that we are headed for a One World Religion is

a _____ _____ _____ _____; or to word it in other

terms, the _____ Movement.   This is designed to "get

rid of any sense of one religion being superior over the other".

This Interfaithism Movement would have people believe that:
- ✓ _____religions are _____ pathways to God.
- ✓ We just need to respect, _____ one another.
- ✓ We need to find common ground with one another.

- Jesus didn't tolerate other faiths. In fact, what was one of the most intolerant statements that He made to the people of His day?

Answer: John 14:6 "I am the way and the truth and the life. No one comes to the Father except through me."

- How can we really "get along" with the following beliefs and the people who adhere to them?

  ✓ That the world was created by the blood of an _____ .

  ✓ That we will burn in a mythical limbo place to purge away our sins before we go to heaven.

  ✓ That we ourselves are gods.

  ✓ That sin and evil is just an illusion

  ✓ That hell is only make believe

  ✓ That heaven for some men will be to endlessly satisfy this lust with as many virgins as they want.

The answer to the above question is obvious, especially when we are told by God to separate from them:

2 Corinthians 6:17-17 states, "Don't team up with those who are unbelievers. How can goodness be a partner with wickedness? How can light live with darkness? What harmony can there be between Christ and the Devil? How can a believer be a partner with an unbeliever? And what union can there be between God's temple and idols? For we are the temple of the living God. As God said: 'I will live in them and walk among them. I will be their God, and they will be my people. Therefore, come out from them and separate yourselves from them, says the Lord."

- Who is really behind the religious, media and political push for the acceptance of this Interfaithism Movement?

Answer: The New Age Occult

The New Agers believe that once all the world's religions come together   "a
_____ leader will be chosen to be earth's religions spokesman
and will then encourage all people of the world to accept a new
_____ leader".

Sounds just like Revelation 13:11-15: "Then I saw another beast come up out of
the earth. He had two horns like those of a lamb, and he spoke with the voice of a
dragon. He exercised all the authority of the first beast. And he required all the
earth and those who belong to this world to worship the first beast, whose death-
wound had been healed. He did astounding miracles, such as making fire flash
down to earth from heaven while everyone was watching. And with all the
miracles he was allowed to perform on behalf of the first beast, he deceived all
the people who belong to this world. He ordered the people of the world to make
a great statue of the first beast, who was fatally wounded and then came back to
life. He was permitted to give life to this statue so that it could speak. Then the
statue commanded that anyone refusing to worship it must die."

The occultic leaders don't believe that this can actually take place until "the
people who will _____ go along with this One World Religion are
_____ the way", or in their own words, when the "elect leave this
dimension as if going to another room". (Sounds like the Rapture!)

People, all over the world, are waiting for the church to disappear "so they can
then be _____ in a One World Religion."

The sign of a One World Religion is a present proof that Christ's Second Coming
is rapidly approaching.

Jesus Himself told His people what to do when you see these things happening:

Luke 21:28: "When these things begin to take place, stand up and lift up your heads, because your redemption is drawing near."

Time is counting down to that exact moment when Jesus returns for His own. If it happened today, would **you** be ready to meet Him as your Friend and Savior, or as your Foe and Judge?

Make sure before it's too late!

Chapter Eight

One World Government

"There was a tough old cowboy who once counseled his grandson that if he wanted to live a long life, the secret was to sprinkle a little gunpowder on his oatmeal every morning.

So respecting the wisdom of his grandfather, the grandson did this religiously every single day of his life. And sure enough he lived to the ripe old age of 93.

In fact, when he died, he left 14 children, 28 grandchildren, 35 great grandchildren and a fifteen-foot hole in the wall of the crematorium."[1]

Now, that guy's hopes for a long life had an explosive ending, didn't it? But do you know what? He's not alone. You see, many people's lives are also headed for an explosive ending. Except it's not going to be from digesting gunpowder. It's going to be from disregarding God's message of grace for the forgiveness of sins in order to be saved. And because of this, people are sadly running the risk of being left behind and will be catapulted into the seven-year Tribulation that is coming upon the whole world.

And folks, the time of the Tribulation is not a party. Jesus said in **Matthew 24** that it would be a time of greater horror than anything the world has ever seen or will ever see again. He also said that unless that time of calamity is shortened, the entire human race would be destroyed. But God is not only a God of wrath; He's a God of love as well. And **because He loves you and I**, He has given us many warning signs so that we would know when the Tribulation could be near and that Christ's 2nd Coming is rapidly approaching. Therefore, to make sure our lives don't have an explosive ending by being left behind, we're going to continue taking a look at **The Final Countdown**.

We already saw how the **#10** sign on **The Final Countdown** was **The Jewish People**. The **#9** sign was **Modern Technology**. The **#8** sign was **Worldwide Upheaval**. The **#7** sign was **The Rise of Falsehood**. The **#6** sign was **The Rise of Wickedness**. The **#5** sign was **The Rise of Apostasy**. In the last chapter we saw how the **#4** sign was none other than **A One World Religion**. There we saw that God lovingly foretold you and I that when we see a worldwide worship of the antichrist, that this would be an indicator that we are in the last days. And isn't that what we see **today**, through the watering down of the truth, the worldwide assault on Christians, and the welcoming of all faiths?

But that's not the only signs that God has given us. The **#3** sign on **The Final Countdown** is none other than **A One World Government**. So just what are these specific prophesies being fulfilled today concerning **A One World Government**, revealing that we could be in the last days? Well, I'm glad you asked. Let's take a look. The **1st End Time Prophecy** concerning **A One World Government** is that **there will be a worldwide authority of the antichrist**.

Revelation 13:2,3,6,7 "And I saw a beast coming out of the sea. He had ten horns and seven heads, with ten crowns on his horns, and on each head a blasphemous name. The dragon gave the beast his power and his throne and great authority. One of the heads of the beast seemed to have had a fatal wound, but the fatal wound had been healed.

The whole world was astonished and followed the beast. He opened his mouth to blaspheme God, and to slander his name and his dwelling place and those who live in heaven. He was given power to make war against the saints and to conquer them. And he was given authority over every tribe, people, language and nation." (NIV)

According to this passage of Scripture, there is coming a day when all the inhabitants of the earth will be under the authority of the antichrist himself. One day, the whole world will be unified into **A One World Government** that is actually **satanically inspired**. But the question is, "Could that really happen?" Could the whole world really be deceived into creating **A One World Government**? And is there any evidence that this is really going to take place just like the Bible said? You bet there is! Let's take a look.

The **1st way** we know that we are headed for **A One World Government** is due to a **Universal Congress**. That's right, I'm talking about the **New World Order**. You see, if you're going to deceive people into creating **A One World Government** then you must certainly provide a **Universal Congress** so that you can dictate a universal compliance, right? And this is precisely what the United Nations and its promotion of a New World Order has been working towards for decades. **Right now** there is waiting for approval, or **already in place**, the plans for **absolute global control of the whole world**. And the tactics that they are using to pull it off are fear and manipulation.

You see, if you're going to get people to surrender their freedoms, then you must get them into a state of fear. Why? Because we are more apt to surrender our freedoms in times of fear than in peace. Therefore, if you create a crisis, you can manage the outcome however you like. This is precisely what's happening to our country. For instance, in order to drum up fear, we are being told that we have a "health-care crisis," a "child care crisis," an "economy crisis," a "constitutional crisis," a "terrorist crisis," and of course, an "environmental crisis."[2] We don't have problems anymore, everything is a horrible crisis just waiting to explode! And because we have been manipulated into a state of fear by all these supposed crisis, we have been prepped to usher in a cry for a universal government to fix all these crisis that are seemingly out of control.

But you might ask, "Come on, does this fear tactic really work on people?" You bet it does. That's why, **right now**, there's a **Universal Law** of the land called the **Earth Charter**, which is a new universal law being used to unite all peoples of the world in order to save the Earth.[3] But wait a minute. If you're going to have a universal law of the land, then you need a **Universal Governing Body** to oversee this law, right? That's why **right now** there's a document called **The Constitution for the Federation Earth**, with plans for a World Government, World Supreme Court, World Capitols, and a World Police.[4] And the only thing holding it up is ratification, which they are hoping will take place real soon. But wait a minute. If you're going to have a universal governing body then you need a **Universal Judicial System** to make sure people obey this World Government, right? And that's why, **right now**, there's a **World Criminal Court**, which went into effect **July of 2002**, thanks in part to the signing of the treaty by Bill Clinton on his last day in office.[5] But wait a minute. If you're going to have a universal judicial system then you need a **Universal Army** to punish those who don't obey this World Government, right? And that's why, **right now**, Tony Blair, the former British Prime Minister, has been calling for **NATO** to become the future "military arm of a new world order rather than strictly a defensive alliance."[6] And if you think about it, haven't we already seen NATO exercise more and more military force over the sovereignty of nations such as Kosovo and Iraq? Hmmm. I wonder who's next?

But you might think, "Come on! This is just too far out. This is just a bunch of wacko conspiracy theories. There's no way the leaders in the world can really be serious about forming **A One World Government**." Well, don't just take my word for it, let's look at theirs:

- **Henry Kissinger** "Today America would be outraged if UN troops entered Los Angeles to restore order. Tomorrow they will be grateful. When presented with this scenario, individual rights will be willingly relinquished for the guarantee of their well-being granted to them by the World Government."

- **David Rockefeller** "We are grateful to the Washington Post, The New York Times, Time Magazine and other great publications whose directors have attended our meetings and respected their promises of discretion for almost forty years. It would have been impossible for us to develop our plan for the world if we had been subject to the bright lights of publicity during those years. But the work is now much more sophisticated and prepared to march towards a world government."

- **Strobe Talbot** (Clinton's Deputy Secretary of State) "In the next century, nations as we know it will be obsolete; all states will recognize a single, global authority. National sovereignty wasn't such a great idea after all."

- **Richard Falk** "The existing order is breaking down at a rapid rate and the main uncertainty is whether mankind can exert a positive role in shaping a new world order...We believe a new order will be born no later than early in the next century..."

- **Mikhail Gorbachev** "Further global progress is now possible only through a quest for universal consensus in the movement towards a new world order."

- **Nelson Mandela** "The new world order that is in the making must focus on the creation of a world democracy, peace and prosperity for all."

- **George McGovern** "I would support a Presidential candidate who pledged to take the following steps...At the end of the war in the Persian

Gulf, press for a comprehensive Middle East settlement and for a new world order based not on Pax Americana but on peace through law with a stronger UN and World Court."

- **George Bush Sr.** "If we do not follow the dictates of our inner moral compass and stand up for human life, then his lawlessness will threaten the peace and democracy of the emerging new world order we now see, this long dreamed-of vision we've all worked toward for so long."

- **Madeleine Albright** "Today I say that no nation in the world need be left out of the global system we are constructing."

- **Mikhail Gorbachev** "The victims of the September 11th attacks will not have died in vain if world leaders use the crisis to create a new world order."

- **Robert Muller** (Former assistant Attorney General of the U.N.) "We must move as quickly as possible to a one-world government; one-world religion; under a one-world leader."[7]

Now, I don't know about you guys, but it sure sounds like somebody is taking this **One World Government** very seriously, how about you? Just like the Bible said. When? In the last days!

The **2nd way** we know that we are headed for **A One World Government** is because of a **Universal Behavior**. That's right, I'm talking about **A New World Community**. You see, if you're going to deceive people into creating **A One World Government** then you must certainly provide a **Universal Standard of Behavior** so that you can dictate a universal compliance, right? And this is precisely what the United Nations has been working towards for decades. Once again they are using fear to manipulate people into surrendering their freedoms.

For instance, in order to preserve our supposed endangered earth, **right now** thanks to the **World Heritage Protection** program, the UN has full authority over millions of acres of land right here in America.[8] Such areas include Yellowstone National Park, the Statue of Liberty, the Grand Canyon, and the Yosemite Valley, just to name a few. Then, in order to preserve our supposed endangered food supply, **right now** the **World Food Summit** continues to meet to govern what crops we can grow, what livestock we can raise and even what we get to eat.[9] Oh, but that's not all. In order to preserve our supposed endangered air, land, and water supply, **right now** the **Agenda for the 21st Century** has plans to dictate our total behavior.[10] What behavior you ask? Well, only what job we get, what housing we have, what education and health care we get, what means of transport, and even how many children we can have. Oh, but it gets worse. In order to preserve our supposed endangered animals, **right now** the **Biodiversity Treaty** is gearing up to dictate where you and I get to live and where the animals get to live.[11] And if that wasn't bad enough, in order to preserve our supposed endangered population, **right now** the **Global Diversity Assessment** has plans to reduce the world's population by eighty percent.[12] And this is precisely why there has been a promotion of feminism, birth control, homosexuality, and abortion. This is why diseases, genocide, and forced sterilization are allowed to continue. Why? Because they all have one thing in common. They all effectively reduce the population. In fact, abortion alone is now estimated to have killed **one billion** lives.[13]

But you might think, "Come on! This is just too far out. This is just a bunch of wacko conspiracy theories. There's no way the leaders in the world can really be serious about **reducing the population of the earth**." Well, don't just take my word for it, let's look at theirs:

- **Margaret Sanger** called for, "The elimination of 'human weeds,' for the 'cessation of charity' because it prolonged the lives of the unfit, for the segregation of 'morons, misfits, and the maladjusted,' and for the sterilization of genetically inferior races."

- **David Graber**, a research biologist with the National Park Service said, "We have become a plague upon ourselves and upon the Earth...Until such time as homo sapiens should decide to rejoin nature, some of us can only hope for the right virus to come along."

- **David Pimentel**, a Cornell University Professor said, "The total world population should be no more than 2 billion rather than the current 5.6 billion."

- **Jacques Cousteau** wrote, "The damage people cause to the planet is a function of demographics – it is equal to the degree of development. One American burdens the earth much more than twenty Bangladeshes...This is a terrible thing to say. In order to stabilize world population, we must eliminate 350,000 people per day. It is a horrible thing to say, but it's just as bad not to say it."

- **Bertrand Russell** wrote, "At present the population of the world is increasing...War so far has had no great effect on this increase...I do not pretend that birth control is the only way in which population can be kept from increasing. There are others...If a Black Death could be spread throughout the world once in every generation, survivors could procreate freely without making the world too full...the state of affairs might be somewhat unpleasant, but what of it? Really high-minded people are indifferent to suffering, especially that of others."

- **Dr. Sam Keen**, a New Age writer and philosopher stated, "We must speak far more clearly about sexuality, contraception, about abortion, about values that control the population, because the ecological crisis, in short, is the population crisis. Cut the population by 90% and there aren't enough people left to do a great deal of ecological damage."[14]

And by the way, they are hoping that all of these programs will be fully integrated by 2012.[15] Now I don't know about you guys, but it sure sounds like somebody is taking this **One World Government** very seriously, how about you? Just like the Bible said. When? In the last days!

The **3rd way** we know that we are headed for **A One World Government** is because of a **Universal Big Brother**. That's right, I'm talking about a **New World Surveillance**. You see, if you're going to deceive people into creating **A One World Government** then you must certainly provide a **Universal Monitoring System** so that you can dictate a universal compliance, right? And this is precisely what the United Nations has been working towards for decades.

Thanks in part to recent Executive Orders, the government now has full authority to utilize the new surveillance technology that's out there.[16] So just what kind of new surveillance technology is out there? Hey, I'm glad you asked. Let's take a look at just a few of them:

1. There is now an aerosol spray that makes unopened envelopes transparent so that the contents can be read. It leaves, no smudging or stain.
2. The FBI was recently granted permission for a new program called Digital Storm which foresees the quadrupling of phone tapping over the next decade.
3. Hidden microphones are being put on utility poles and rooftops in Los Angeles to monitor "strange noises."
4. Every square foot of farming land in Australian is now being watched via satellite to monitor food production and crop yields.
5. Here in America, satellites are being used by state governments to search for unreported improvements that might increase property taxes, to check for water-use permits, and to find improper tree cutting.
6. There are currently radar guns using radio waves that can peer through concrete walls and satellites with the same capability are on the way.
7. Government officials can now aim an antenna at your computer monitor, and from the radiation emitted by the monitor, they can reconstruct the images on your screen.
8. Tiny surveillance devices have been developed called "smart dust" which are so small they can float in the air like dust and be suspended by air currents while they are sensing and communicating for hours.[17]

Hmmm. Very interesting isn't it? I'd say somebody wants to keep an eye on things, how about you? And speaking of keeping and eye on us, a USA Today article had this to say about the emergence of so many video surveillance cameras:

"Whether as motorists or pedestrians; as visitors to convenience stores, banks, ATMs or the post office; as shoppers with credit cards or telephone users; even at leisure, in parks, playgrounds and golf courses, we're constantly on candid camera. Full-time surveillance is a reality of modern life."[18]

What? Could full time surveillance really be a modern reality? Look around people and you tell me. All in the name of reducing crime and traffic concerns, millions of cameras are not only going up right here in America, but they've already been in place for a long time and **they're all tied together**. In fact, **right now** you can go to dozens of web sites and "monitor" traffic and people, "just for fun," not only here in America but throughout the globe. However, don't just take my word for it. See for yourself by doing a web search for "online traffic cameras" and you'll see what I mean.

But you might think, "Come on. Surely they would never use them to keep an eye on our every move." But folks, if that's true then why are there, **right now** in England, over **4 million** cameras in the government and private sector which have been dubbed a virtual "surveillance canopy"?[19] And believe it or not, all of this is pretty much common knowledge to the average Britain. In fact, one person had this to say about just how dense this surveillance really is:

"So dense is the network that in many urban areas people may be monitored from the moment they step out of their front door and be kept under observation on their way to work, in the office, and even in a restaurant if they choose to dine out. Over the course of a day they could be filmed by 300 cameras. The latest figures show that, in cities, people are captured on film at least once every five minutes."[20]

Oh, but that's not all. Why do you think that Japan has followed suit with tons of it's own cameras and has even gone so far as to install intercoms on some of their cameras to warn people in advance of inappropriate behavior?[21] And just in case video surveillance doesn't cover all the bases, **right now** there is a Global Project called Echelon that is a cooperative effort among the United States, England, Canada, New Zealand, and Australia. So what does it do? Well, under the guise of national security and terrorist threats, it simply monitors and intercepts all **phone calls, faxes, data transfers, radio transmissions and emails**. How does it work? Well, they simply monitor all transmissions at the rate of two million per hour looking for key words like "terrorize," or "assassination," or even the word "bomb." If any of these and many other "key words" appear in the transmission, a hard copy as well as a recording of the conversation is sent to someone's desk to be analyzed.[22] But you might think, "Come on. This is just more of that wacko conspiracy stuff. This can't be true." Well, don't just take my word for it. Let's listen to Mike Frost who personally worked there, collecting information for nineteen years:

"Communications know no borders. Somebody will pick it up somewhere, and it will end up on somebody's desk...I guarantee it.

Case in point...a lady was on the phone talking to her friend about a school play that she'd been to the night before; her son was in a school play. And she thought he'd done a lousy job, and she said to her friend, 'Boy, he really bombed last night.'

That conversation was highlighted and ended up on an analyst's desk the next morning because the word 'bomb' was in there, and all this lady was doing was talking about her son and his play the night before.

Now that conversation of that lady is held...indefinitely, so if two or three or four years later, she talks about somebody else bombing or something, and the computer spits it out again as being the second or third hit on this person's name, you can graduate from being a possible terrorist to a probable terrorist. It's that easy.

If they say that you are a probable terrorist and passes that information on to those responsible for that sort of activity, just think about what could happen to your life, and you'd never know why.

All of a sudden, your MasterCard doesn't work anymore; All a sudden, your phone is down; all of a sudden, things are falling apart in your life; and you have no reason why, and nobody'll ever tell you.

And he has a warning for anyone who says 'it can't happen to me.'

'If you don't want anybody to know about what you're saying, don't say it. Because if you do say it, somebody will be listening.'"[23]

Now I don't know about you guys, but it sure sounds like somebody is taking this **One World Government** very seriously, how about you? Just like the Bible said. When? In the last days!

However, you might be tempted to think that there's no way that people are going to be able to pull off **A One World Government**. Nobody's ever going to fall for this or ever let it happen. But folks, it's not only **going to be put into place**, it's been in the planning stages for a long time. Here, see the progress for yourself:

1. 1913: The League of Nations was formed
2. 1919: The Council on Foreign Relations was formed
3. 1922: The CFR endorses World Government
4. 1945: The United Nations was formed
5. 1948: The World Constitution is drafted providing a World Council to enforce World Law and calls upon nations to surrender their arms to a World Government
6. 1959: The Diagram of World Government under the Constitution for the Federation of Earth is developed
7. 1967: Richard Nixon calls for a New World Order
8. 1968: Nelson Rockefeller pledges support of the New World Order

9. 1970: Education and mass media begin to promote a New World Order
10. 1972: The first draft completed of The Constitution for the Federation of Earth
11. 1988: Mikhail Gorbachev speaks of a New World Order
12. 1990: George Bush Sr. speaks of a New World Order
13. 1992: The Earth Summit is held and produces the Biodiversity treaty and Agenda 21
14. 1993: Bill Clinton speaks of a New World Order
15. 1995: Foreign troops begin training on American soil
16. 1995: The term New World Order is replaced with Global Governance
17. 1995: The State of the World Forums begin and continue yearly in San Franciso
18. 1996: The World Food Summit is held
19. 2000: The Millennium Assembly and Summit held at U.N. and studies how to implement Global Governance
20. 2000: The Earth Charter is created (A New Universal Law)
21. 2000: The State of the World Forum meets to advance Global Governance
22. 2001: A celebration for the Earth Charter is held and placed in The Ark of Hope (similar replica of the Biblical ark)
23. 2001: Tom Brokaw (popular US news anchor) announces the world now has formed into the New World Order.
24. 2002: The Earth Charter is brought to the U.N.
25. 2002: A World Criminal Court is ratified and begins
26. 2002: The Earth Charter is expected to be endorsed at the next World Summit
27. 2002: FDA approves VeriChip Microchip implant for humans
28. 2003: The EU plans to include facial and fingerprint biometric data on travel documents for non-EU foreign nationals by 2005
29. 2003: Britain takes a dramatic step towards a fully-fledged European army with EU.
30. 2003: UN discusses whether an international body such as the United Nations should be in charge of running the Internet
31. 2003: Microchips are proposed to keep children safe.
32. 2004: Pope calls for a New World Order
33. 2004: Chips implanted in cop's hand would allow only officer to fire the gun
34. 2004: Library board approves microchips to track books
35. 2004: Call for a national ID with driver's licenses

36. 2004: Bill Clinton proposed to run U.N.
37. 2004: Bush Calls for New World Order
38. 2004:CFR proposes the establishment by 2010 of a North American Union with a common currency called the amero
39. 2005: Proposed that Europe lead the World
40. 2005: Pope Invites Nations to Establish Ties
41. 2005: Compulsory ID cards proposed in Europe
42. 2005: Bush signs the REAL ID Act that requires people entering federal buildings, boarding airplanes or opening bank accounts to present natonal identification via driver's licenses
43. 2005: China and Russia call for a New World Order
44. 2005: National ID system proposed in Australia
45. 2005: Britain will be first country to monitor every car journey
46. 2005: Pope Calls for New World Order
47. 2005: Project Alpha envisions by 2025 fighting force that is largely robotic
48. 2006: Blair calls for a New World Order
49. 2006: Bush joins talks to create a North American Union
50. 2006: Google is projected to keep tabs on all people
51. 2007: Mexico's Fox openly calls for North American Union
52. 2007: North American union plan headed to Congress in fall
53. 2007: Prior to taking office as British Prime Minister, Gordon Brown talks of a New World Order
54. 2007: EU vows to shape globalization
55. 2007: FBI aims for world's largest biometrics database
56. 2008: British Prime Minister Gordon Brown talks with other world leaders on far-reaching reform of the United Nations Security Council as part of a drive to create a "new world order" and "global society"
57. 2008: Blair announces he'll be president of Europe if given the power
58. 2008: North American Army created between U.S. & Canada without Congressional approval
59. 2011: The national REAL ID card goes into effect
60. 2015: The World Food Summit's goal to reduce ½ half the number of undernourished people (one of many methods is via population control)[24]

Now, how many of you have heard about these events on the news lately? Of course not! In fact, these people who are pushing for **A One World Government** have already begun to celebrate by establishing a monument right here in America. In Elberton County, Georgia stands the Georgia Guidestones, which is a stone monolith similar to Stonehenge. And in eight different languages is written Ten Guides or Commandments for the world:

1. Maintain humanity under 500,000,000 in perpetual balance with nature.
2. Guide reproduction wisely – improving fitness and diversity.
3. Unite humanity with a living new language.
4. Rule passion – faith – tradition – and all things with tempered reason.
5. Protect people and nations with fair laws and just courts.
6. Let all nations rule internally resolving external disputes in a world court.
7. Avoid petty laws and useless officials.
8. Balance personal rights with social duties.
9. Prize truth – beauty – love – seeking harmony with the infinite.
10. Be not a cancer on the earth – Leave room for nature – Leave room for nature.[25]

Now I don't know about you guys, but it sure sounds like somebody is taking this **One World Government** very seriously, how about you? Oh, by the way, a reduction of the world's population would require the annihilation of ninety percent of the world's population. Hmmm. That kind of sounds like the mass extermination of the earth's population during the time of the tribulation.

Revelation 9:15,18,20 "And the four angels who had been prepared for this hour and day and month and year were turned loose to kill one-third of all the people on earth. One-third of all the people on earth were killed by these three plagues – by the fire and the smoke and burning sulfur. But the people who did not die in these plagues still refused to turn from their evil deeds." (NLT)

Hmmm. You mean there could actually come a time when the world would not even be shocked at the death of millions of people on the planet? That would be, uh huh. In fact, many people today would welcome that sort of thing, wouldn't they? And maybe it's because people are increasingly convinced that this kind of holocaust is actually a good thing is also one of the reasons why many will refuse to repent and turn to God. But could that really happen? People, it's already happening before our very eyes. When? In the last days.

And believe it or not, even with all this amazing evidence pointing to the signs of Christ's soon return, some people still have no clue as to what's causing all the pain in the world, like this lady:

"One day a lady was throwing a party for her granddaughter, and she had gone all out. She hired a caterer, a band, and even a clown. But just before the party started, two bums showed up looking for a handout. And so feeling sorry for them the woman told them that she would give them a meal if they will help chop some wood for her. They gratefully agreed and headed to the rear of the house where the wood was.

Meanwhile the guests arrived, and all was going well with the children having a wonderful time. But there was one problem. The clown hadn't shown up. Then after a half an hour, the clown finally called to report that he was stuck in traffic, and would probably not make the party at all.

At this the woman was very disappointed and unsuccessfully tried to entertain the children herself. And just when she was about to give up hope, she happened to look out the window and saw one of the bums doing cartwheels across the lawn. In fact, she continued to watch in awe as he swung from tree branches, did midair flips, and leaped high in the air.

So the lady spoke to the other bum and said, 'What your friend is doing is absolutely marvelous. I have never seen such a thing. Do you think your friend would consider repeating this performance for the children at the party? In fact, I would pay him $50!'

So the other bum says, 'Well, I dunno. Let me ask him. HEY WILLIE! FOR $50, WOULD YOU CHOP OFF ANOTHER TOE?'"[26]

Now, that lady was totally clueless about that guy's pain, wasn't she? She had no idea about what was really taking place. But you know what? She's not alone. You see, many people today think that their lives are going to become pain free and a virtual paradise through **A One World Government**. They think they can once and for all get rid of God's authority and rule themselves. Yet they are totally clueless about what's really taking place. The Bible says that God is not only laughing at them, but that He will also soon rebuke those who reject His authority over their lives.

Psalm 2:1-5 "Why do the nations rage? Why do the people waste their time with futile plans? The kings of the earth prepare for battle; the rulers plot together against the LORD and against his anointed one. 'Let us break their chains,' they cry, 'and free ourselves from this slavery.' But the one who rules in heaven laughs. The Lord scoffs at them. Then in anger he rebukes them, terrifying them with his fierce fury." (NLT)

People of God, I hope you're not one of those who have bought into this lie that man can somehow provide his own paradise by creating **A One World Government**. Why? Because you might wake up one day and discover that **you've been left behind**. Please, I beg you, get right with God **now** before it's too late! And whatever you do, don't be like one of those people who say something like this. "Okay, I'm not going to accept Jesus right now, but if I see you Christians disappear in this rapture thing, I'll know it was true and I'll get saved then." Are you kidding me? Don't you realize that if you wait until the Tribulation to get saved it will cost you your head **literally**! I didn't say that. God did!

Revelation 20:4 "And I saw the souls of those who had been beheaded because of their testimony for Jesus and because of the word of God. They had not worshiped the beast or his image and had not received his mark on their foreheads or their hands." (NIV)

People, stop kidding yourself. If you won't get saved now when it's still relatively easy to be a Christian, you mean to tell me you will when you're literally threatened with getting your head chopped off! Stop lying to yourself! Wouldn't it make much more sense to get saved now and avoid the Wrath to come? Please, I beg you, get right with God now! And here's the great news. God doesn't want you left behind. Because He loves you and I, He has given us the warning sign of **A One World Government** to show us that the Tribulation **could be near** and that Christ's 2nd Coming is rapidly approaching. Jesus Himself said this:

Luke 21:28 "When these things begin to take place, stand up and lift up your heads, because your redemption is drawing near." (NIV)

Like it or not folks, we are headed for **The Final Countdown**. We don't know the day or the hour. Only God knows. The point is, if you're a Christian, it's time to get up off our blessed assurance and get bold for Almighty God! Folks, it's high time we Christians speak up and declare the good news of salvation to those who are dying all around us. But please, if you're not a Christian, give your life to Jesus today, because tomorrow may be too late! Just like the Bible said!

Study Questions

Review

Jesus Christ is returning very soon! The signs that indicate this to be true are overwhelming in these last days.

- Can you remember what they've been so far?

Sign #10 was The _____People

Sign # 9 was Modern _____

Sign # 8 was _____Upheaval

Sign #7 was The Rise of _____

Sign #6 was The Rise of _____

Sign #5 was The Rise of_____

Sign #4 was A One World _____

- Pastor Billy shared three indicators that the world is shaping up for a One World Religion. Can you recall them?

1. A _____ _____ of the truth.
2. A worldwide assault on _____.
3. A _____ of _____faiths.

This Chapter:

The #3 sign of the Final Countdown is none other than a One World

_____ that will be under the authority of the

_____ .

Revelation 13:2,3,6,7; "And I saw a beast coming out of the sea. He had ten horns and seven heads, with ten crowns on his horns, and on each head a blasphemous name. The dragon gave the beast his power and his throne and great authority. One of the heads of the beast seemed to have had a fatal wound, but the fatal wound had been healed. The whole world was astonished and followed the beast. He opened his mouth to blaspheme God, and to slander his name and his dwelling place and those who live in heaven. He was given power to make war against the saints and to conquer them. And he was given authority over every tribe, people, language and nation."

- How do we know today that we are headed in the direction of a One World Government? Are there any indicators?

THE 1ST WAY

The first way that we are headed for a One World Government is due to a
_____ _____ or to put it in other terms: The New World
_____. Right now there is waiting for approval, or already in place, the plans for _____ global _____ of the whole world.

- What are the tactics they are using to pull it off?
Answer: _____ and _____ .

If you create a crisis you can manage the outcome however you like. And so, that's exactly what's happening to our country. In order to create fear in people, we are being told that we have:

✓ a "_____ - _____ crisis"

✓ a "_____-care crisis"

✓ an "_____ crisis"

✓ a "_____ crisis"

✓ a "_____ crisis"

✓ an "_____ crisis"

• Does this fear tactic work?

Answer:
    ✓ Right now, there's a Universal Law of the land called the Earth _____.

    ✓ Right now, there's a document called The _____ for the _____ Earth, with plans for;

✓ World _____

✓ World _____ Court

✓ World _____

    ✓ Right now, there's a World _____ Court, which went into effect July of 2002.

If you're going to have a universal judicial system then you need a Universal _____ to punish those who don't obey this World Government. All of this and more is happening **RIGHT NOW!**

Tony Blair, the former British Prime Minister, called for _____ to become the future "military army of a new world order...."

If you don't think our world leaders are seriously thinking of forming a One World Government, then listen to these quotes:

- **Henry Kissinger:** "Today America would be outraged if UN troops entered Los Angeles to restore order. Tomorrow they will be grateful. When presented with this scenario, individual rights will be willingly relinquished for the guarantee of their well-being granted to them by the World Government."

- **David Rockefeller:** "We are grateful to the Washington Post, The New York Times, Time Magazine and other great publications whose directors have attended our meetings and respected their promises of discretion for almost forty years. It would have been impossible for us to develop our plan for the world if we had been subject to the bright lights of publicity during those years. But the work is now much more sophisticated and prepared to march towards a world government."

- **Strobe Talbot** (Clinton's Deputy Secretary of State): "In the next century, nations as we know it will be obsolete; all states will recognize a single, global authority. National sovereignty wasn't such a great idea after all."

- **Richard Falk:** "The existing order is breaking down at a rapid rate and the main uncertainty is whether mankind can exert a positive role in shaping a new world order...We believe a new order will be born no later than early in the next century..."

- **Mikhail Gorbachev:** "Further global progress is now possible only through a quest for universal consensus in the movement towards a new world order."

- **Nelson Mandela:** "The new world order that is in the making must focus on the creation of a world democracy, peace and prosperity for all."

- **George McGovern:** "I would support a Presidential candidate who pledged to take the following steps…At the end of the war in the Persian Gulf, press for a comprehensive Middle East settlement and a new world order based not on Pax Americana but on peace through law with a stronger UN and World Court."

- **George Bush Sr.:** "If we do not follow the dictates of our inner moral compass and stand up for human life, then his lawlessness will threaten the peace and democracy of the emerging new world order we now see, this long dreamed-of vision we've all worked toward for so long."

- **Madeleine Albright:** "Today I say that no nation in the world need be left out of the global system we are constructing."

- **Mikhail Gorbachev:** "The victims of the September 11th attacks will not have died in vain if world leaders use the crisis to create a new world order."

- **Robert Muller** (Former assistant Attorney General of the U.N.): "We must move as quickly as possible to a one-world government; one-world religion; under a one-world leader."

THE 2ND WAY

The second way we know that we are headed for a One World Government is because of a Universal _____ _____ or to put it in other terms, a New World _____, or a Universal _____ System.

What kind of new surveillance technology is out there?

1. There is now an aerosol spray that makes unopened envelopes transparent so that the contents can be read. It leaves, no smudging or stain.

2. The FBI was recently granted permission for a new program called Digital Storm which foresees the quadrupling of phone tapping over the next decade.

3. Hidden microphones are being put on utility poles and rooftops in Los Angeles to monitor "strange noises."

4. Every square foot of farming land in Australia is now being watched via satellite to monitor food production and crop yields.

5. Here in America, satellites are being used by state governments to search for unreported improvements that might increase property taxes, to check for water-use permits, and to find improper tree cutting.

6. There are currently radar guns using radio waves that can peer through concrete walls and satellites with the same capability are on the way.

7. Government officials can now aim an antenna at your computer monitor, and from the radiation emitted by the monitor, they can reconstruct the images on your screen.

8. Tiny surveillance devices have been developed called "smart dust" which is so small they can float in the air like dust and be suspended by air currents while they are sensing and communicating for hours.

Right now there is a Global Project called _____ that is a cooperative effort among the United States, _____, _____, New Zealand, and _____. Echelon monitors and intercepts all:

✓ _____ calls
✓ faxes
✓ _____ transfers
✓ _____transmissions
✓ emails

It monitors all transmissions at a rate of two million per hour looking for such key words like, "_____," or "_____," or even the word, "_____."

If any of these "key words" appear in the transmission, a hard copy as well as a recording of the conversation is sent to someone's desk to be analyzed.

• Are you saying, 'this can't be true'?

Answer: Listen to Mike Frost who personally worked there, collecting information for nineteen years:

"Communications know no borders. Somebody will pick it up somewhere, and it will end up on somebody's desk…I guarantee it.

Case in point…a lady was on the phone talking to her friend about a school play that she'd been to the night before; her son was in a school play. And she thought he'd done a lousy job, and she said to her friend, "Boy, he really bombed last night." The conversation was highlighted and ended up on the analyst's desk the next morning because the word 'bomb' was in there, and all this lady was doing was talking about her son and his play the night before.

Now that conversation of that lady is held…indefinitely, so if two or three or four years later, she talks about somebody else bombing or something, and the computer spits it out again as being the second or third hit on this person's name, you can graduate from being a possible terrorist to a probable terrorist. It's that easy.

If they say that you are a probable terrorist and pass that information on to those responsible for that sort of activity, just think about what could happen to your life, and you'd never know why.

All of a sudden, your MasterCard doesn't work anymore; all of a sudden, your phone is done; all of a sudden, things are falling apart in your life; and you have no reason why, and nobody will ever tell you.

And he has a warning for anyone who says 'it can't happen to me.' If you don't want anybody to know about what you're saying, don't say it, because if you do say it, somebody will be listening."

No doubt about it! God has also given us this warning sign of a One World _____ to show us that Christ's 2nd Coming is rapidly approaching.

Jesus encouraged His Church with these words:

Luke 21:28 "When these things begin to take place, stand up and lift up your heads, because your redemption is drawing near."

Are you ready to meet God the Son?

Chapter Nine

One World Economy

Hey, how many of you guys out there have noticed that the news media is just a little biased when it comes to reporting Christian events? Anyone besides me? So, just to make sure we're all on the same page here, I'm going to show you just how bad this media assault has become against Christianity by applying their current standards of biased journalism to past Biblical events. You tell me just how accurate these headlines might indeed be:

1. The Crossing of the Red Sea would be reported as:
   WETLANDS TRAMPLED IN LABOR STRIKE (Pursuing Environmentalists Killed)

2. David vs. Goliath would be reported as:
   HATE CRIME KILLS BELOVED CHAMPION (Psychologist Questions the Influence of Rock)

3. Elijah on Mt. Carmel would be reported as:
   FIRE SENDS RELIGIOUS RIGHT EXTREMIST INTO FRENZY (400 People Killed)

4. The birth of Jesus would be reported as:

HOTELS FULL, ANIMALS LEFT HOMELESS (Animal Rights Activists Enraged by Insensitive Couple)

5. The feeding of the 5,000 would be reported as:
   PREACHER STEALS CHILD'S LUNCH (Disciples Mystified Over Behavior)

6. The healing of the 10 lepers would be reported as:
   LOCAL DOCTOR'S PRACTICE RUINED ("Faith Healer" Causes Bankruptcy)

7. The healing of the Gadarene demoniac would be reported as:
   MADMAN'S FRIEND CAUSES STAMPEDE (Local Farmer's Investment Lost)

8. Raising Lazarus from the dead would be reported as:
   FUNDAMENTALIST PREACHER RAISES A STINK (Will Reading to be Delayed)[1]

Now, how many of you believe that that's pretty accurate as to how things would be reported today? Uh huh. It's not too far off is it? And it's all because the world is getting more and more biased and antagonistic towards Christianity and the truth that we proclaim of God's salvation from sin and the destruction to come. But the sad thing is that, as long as they continue to do this, they are running the risk of being left behind, which means that they will be catapulted into the seven-year Tribulation that is coming upon the whole world.

And folks, the time of the Tribulation is not a party. Jesus said in **Matthew 24** that it would be a time of greater horror than anything the world has ever seen or will ever see again. He also said that unless that time of calamity is shortened, the entire human race would be destroyed. But God is not only a God of wrath; He's a God of love as well. And **because He loves you and I**, He has given us many warning signs so that we would know when the Tribulation could be near and that Christ's 2nd Coming is rapidly approaching. Therefore, to make sure we're well informed about the dangers of being left behind, we're going to continue taking a look at **The Final Countdown**.

We already saw how the **#10** sign on **The Final Countdown** was **The Jewish People**. The **#9** sign was **Modern Technology**. The **#8** sign was **Worldwide Upheaval**. The **#7** sign was **The Rise of Falsehood**. The **#6** sign was **The Rise of Wickedness**. The **#5** sign was **The Rise of Apostasy**. The **#4** sign was a **One World Religion**. In the last chapter we saw how the **#3** sign was none other than **A One World Government**. There we saw that God lovingly foretold you and I that when we see a worldwide authority of the antichrist, that this would be an indicator that we are in the last days. Isn't that what we see **today**, by a push for a new world order, new world community and a new world surveillance system?

But that's not the only signs that God has given us. The **#2** sign on **The Final Countdown** is none other than **A One World Economy**. So just what are these specific prophesies being fulfilled today concerning **A One World Economy**, revealing that we could be in the last days? Well, I'm glad you asked. Let's take a look. The **1st** End Time Prophecy concerning **A One World Economy** is that **there will be a worldwide economy of the antichrist**.

Revelation 13:11,12,16,17 "Then I saw another beast come up out of the earth. He exercised all the authority of the first beast. And he required all the earth and those who belong to this world to worship the first beast. He required everyone – great and small, rich and poor, slave and free – to be given a mark on the right hand or on the forehead. And no one could buy or sell anything without that mark." (NLT)

According to this passage of Scripture, there is coming a day when all the inhabitants of the earth will be under the economy of the antichrist himself, who controls all buying and selling. One day, the whole world will be unified into **A One World Economy** that is actually **satanically inspired**. But the question is, "Could that really happen?" Could the whole world really be deceived into creating **A One World Economy**? And is there any evidence that this is really going to take place just like the Bible said? You bet there is! Let's take a look.

The **1ˢᵗ way** we know that we are headed for **A One World Economy** is due to a **Universal Banking System**. That's right, I'm talking about a **Global Bank**. You see, if you're going to deceive people into creating **A One World Economy** then you must certainly provide a **Universal Bank** so that you can dictate a universal monetary exchange, right? Well, guess what? That's precisely what's happening. **Right now** there are **already in place** the plans for **absolute economic control of the whole world**. How do I know? Because **right now** there's **already** a **Universal Bank**, called the **World Bank** which is the world's leading lender of money to the nations around the globe.[2] But wait a minute. If you're going to have a universal bank then you need a **Universal Lending Institution** to oversee the dispersion of money and loans, right? Well gee, guess what? That's why **right now** the **International Monetary Fund** oversees the whole world's financial system and even fixes the exchange rates.[3] But wait a minute. If you're going to have a universal lending institution then you need a **Universal Money Exchanger** to appropriately funnel all this money to all the different countries, right? Well gee, guess what? **Right now** there's a **Universal Electronic Banking System** called **SWIFT**, which automatically makes sure that all the different money transactions in the world match all the different currencies.[4] But wait a minute. If you're going to have a universal money exchanger then you need to have a **Universal Strong Arm** to punish those who don't obey this World Banking System, right? Well gee, guess what? **Right now** there's the **World Trade Organization**, which not only sets the trading rules for the world, but punishes all countries who do not obey with billion dollar fines and sanctions. It even happens here in America.[5]

And lest you think that people aren't serious about forming this one world economy, with the birth of the Euro we see for the first time, a multitude of nations coming under one unified currency.[6] In fact, people like Tony Blair, the former Prime Minister of Britain, are showing signs of support for England to hop on the bandwagon as well.[7] And recently, Robert Mundell, considered the "godfather of the Euro," gave a blueprint for a single world currency, including the U.S., England, and Japan. Since the initial plans for a world currency were shot down by the U.S. more than fifty years ago, Mundell stated this:

"It is now time and useful, and in the United States interest, to move toward (global monetary reform) and provide some leadership. The lessons learned from the creation of the…Euro could help moves toward one world currency."[8]

He also readily agreed that we would probably never go along with this, so he proposed starting with Japan and England and force us into it economically.

But you might think, "Come on! This is just too far out. This is just a coincidence. There's no way the leaders in the world can really be serious about forming **A One World Economy**." But folks, it's not only **going to happen**, it's been in the planning stages for a long time. Here, see the progress for yourself:

1. 1913: The Federal Reserve created (It is neither federal nor a reserve and is owned by banks. It was planned at a secret meeting in 1910 on Jekyl Island, Georgia by a group of bankers and politicians. This transferred the power to create money from the American government to a private group of bankers and thus violates Article I of the Constitution, which states, "Congress shall have the power to coin money and regulate the value thereof." (NOT BANKS!)
2. 1944: The World Bank was formed (world's foremost lender)
3. 1944: (IMF) International Monetary Fund formed (world's overseer of international financial system)

4. 1944: (GATT) General Agreement on Tariffs and Trade (liberalized world trade)
5. 1968: Club of Rome formed (group of economic elite world advisers)
6. 1973: Trilateral commissioned formed by banker David Rockefeller to develop a worldwide economic power.
7. 1973: (SWIFT) Society for Worldwide Interbank Finance Transactions created (universal electronic banking organization that transfers monetary transactions between countries and corporations)
8. 1975: Declaration of Interdependence signed which declares that our economy should be regulated by international authorities.
9. 1979: Smart card developed
10. 1993: Mondex International formed
11. 1994: (NAFTA) North American Free Trade Agreement (free trade between Canada, U.S., and Mexico)
12. 1995: (WTO) world Trade Organization formed (develops and enforces worldwide trade rules)
13. 1999: The Euro is born (new universal currency of 12 European countries)
14. 2002: The first Euro coins and banknotes go into circulation
15. 2002: Call for a Global Tax to be paid to the United Nations at World Conference held in Monterrey, Mexico
16. 2002: Fast Track Bill approved that prevents congress from changing or even having an extended debate on any trade agreement negotiated by the President
17. 2003: Proposal appears for credit card implants
18. 2003: Proposal to keep children safe with a microchip
19. 2003: EU to use to chip to monitor visitors
20. 2004: Biometric payments expanding to grocery and convenience stores
21. 2004: Bank card crimes fuel rush to biometric systems
22. 2004: Baja Beach Club in Barcelona Spain launches microchip implantation for VIP members
23. 2004: Wal-Mart turns on radio tags
24. 2004: Microchip and global satellite firms each agreement
25. 2004: Chirac calls for a global tax
26. 2004: 44,000 prison inmates to be RFID-chipped
27. 2004: Mexico attorney general gets microchip implant
28. 2004: Japan school kids to be tagged with RFID chips
29. 2004: Proposal for chip implanted in police officer's hands to allow only officers to fire guns
30. 2005: House approves electronic ID cards

31. 2005: California school requires radio ID tags for students
32. 2005: Windows to become RFID friendly
33. 2005: The Bank for International Settlements calls for global currency
34. 2005: (FTAA) Free Trade Agreement of the Americas is proposed to provide free trade in the whole Western Hemisphere
35. 2005: Proposal for a Digital Birth ID
36. 2005: Dutch, USA to start airport biometric data checks
37. 2005: Chase launches new microchip blink credit card
38. 2005: Chief of Police who received VeriChip advocates forced government chipping to buy and sell
39. 2005: Scientist calls for world DNA database
40. 2006: Employees get microchip implants
41. 2006: VeriChip sells first Baby Protection System and in talks with Military
42. 2006: Proposed that Britons be microchipped like dogs in a decade
43. 2006: IMF wins new powers to police global economy
44. 2006: Rise of people voluntarily receiving microchips implants
45. 2006: Couples receive implants as a sign of love for each other
46. 2006: Young shoppers want to pay with chip in skin
47. 2007: Invisible RFID Ink available for cattle and people
48. 2007: Proposal for animal tags for people
49. 2007: FBI to collect biometric information on Britons
50. 2007: Russia launches final satellites for its own GPS
51. 2007: FBI aims for world's largest biometrics database
52. 2007: Alzheimer's Patients lining up for microchips
53. 2007: Secret new plan for EU Super State unveiled
54. 2008: Seven year plan aligns U.S. with Europe's economy
55. 2008: Digital Angel keeps tabs on animals
56. 2008: FBI wants instant access to British identity data
57. 2008: Hospitals tagging babies with electronic chips
58. 2008: Prisoners to be chipped like dogs[9]

Now, how many of you have heard about any of that stuff, let alone the coming global tax on the news lately? Of course not! In fact, one article made it clear as to the reasons why:

"The jury is still out on which way the United States will go on the issue of global economic control by the UN. Most Americans will never know the issue is on the table until after the decisions are made. The media is not likely to address the issue, nor is it likely to be a topic of congressional debate. These events are taking place in other parts of the world, with decisions being made by officials who are not elected by anyone. No elected official in the United States has any authority to alter or veto these decisions. The world is moving swiftly toward global governance."[10]

You see, the reason why we probably won't hear about this is because the day we see the passage of the global tax, which the United Nations is calling for **right now**, is the day we officially kick off **A One World Economy**, and by then it will be too late. And correct me if I'm wrong, but I'd say somebody's very serious about forming **A One World Economy**, how about you?

Oh, but that's not all. Little do people know that these same economic powers have already divided up the world into **Ten Economic Kingdoms** in order to assure proper control.[11] Each kingdom will be ruled by an individual dictator who will be under the authority of a world dictator. But you might say, "There's no way that the American people will stand for this. Why, we'll stand up and fight if it comes to that!" Well, they've already thought of that. You see, the plan is to have foreign, not America troops on American soil. Why? Because most likely another American would have a hard time shooting a fellow American, but a foreigner wouldn't!t![12] Hey, wait a minute. Didn't we see how foreign troops were **already being trained** right here in America? Hmmm. I wonder why?

And if that wasn't scary enough, most people still **don't get the significance** of this world division by an Economic Club from Rome. Why? Because most people haven't read the Scripture that talks about the coming Revived Roman Empire, with it's ten-horned kingdom that would appear on the scene. When? In the last days!

Revelation 17:9,12-13 "And now understand this. His ten horns are ten kings who have not yet risen to power; they will be appointed to their kingdoms for one brief moment to reign with the beast. They will all agree to give their power and authority to him." (NLT)

Hey, wait a second. You mean to tell me that there's going to come a day when we see a worldwide kingdom of the antichrist that is split up into ten kingdoms? Could that really happen? Folks, it's happening right before our eyes! What do you think is going on with the birth of the **European Union**? Hello! What's that? Isn't that a **region** of countries coming together **economically** with their own currency called the **Euro**? And why there **right now** the formation of the **African Union** which is a **region** of countries coming together **economically** with their own currency called the **Golden Mandela**, which is supposed to go into affect by 2010?[13] And speaking of 2010, why is there **right now** the formation of the North American Union, which is made up of the United States, Canada and Mexico coming together **economically** with a new currency called the **Amero**?[14] They're shooting for 2010 as well. But that's still not all. There's also plans **right now** for a South American Union, an Asian Union, a Central Asian Union, and even a Pacific Union to name a few.[15] Why, if I didn't know better, I'd say the world is being split up into different economic regions right before our very eyes. Gee, I wonder how many they'll end up with? Maybe, **ten**! Just like the Bible said. When? In the last days.

The **2nd way** we know that we are headed for **A One World Economy** is due to a **Universal Currency**. That's right, I'm talking about the coming **Cashless Society**. You see, if you're going to deceive people into creating **A One World Economy** then you must certainly provide a **Universal Currency** so that you can dictate a universal monetary standard, right? Well gee, guess what? That's precisely what's happening.

You see, in case you haven't noticed, we have slowly but surely moved towards a completely cashless society. **In the last century alone**, we have gone from **paper currency to electronic cash**. For instance, if we don't have any money on us, don't worry, just **write a check**. Then, if we don't have the money to write a check, don't worry, just charge it to **a credit card**. But if we don't want to pay the interest on a credit card, don't worry, just take it out of your checking account with **a debit card**.

And now all these features and more are **all combined into one**, called a **smart card**. And these smart cards are now being hailed as "digital cash" or "electronic purses." In fact, experts say that **these smart cards will soon be the world's first truly universal currency**. So what in the world is a smart card? Well, I'm glad you asked. A smart card is about the size of a regular credit card only it **has a tiny microchip** that can store and receive information. And because of this feature, you can use them for all kinds of things. Let's take a look:

1. Personal ATM
2. Purchases (at stores, restaurants, vending machines, gas, toll roads, etc.)
3. Telephone calls
4. Access to cable and satellite programs
5. Internet purchases
6. Vehicle and building access
7. Personal computer access (replace all passwords)
8. Loyalty programs (airlines, grocery stores, etc.)
9. Rapid Check-in (hotels, airlines, etc.)
10. Personal Identification Holder (Soc. Security, Driver's License, Student ID, Health and Insurance ID, voting information, picture, and fingerprints)[16]

Hey now, who couldn't use a little more convenience and flexibility in their busy lives, huh? In fact, imagine if we could get rid of all paper currency. Smart cards could even reduce fear by spelling the beginning of the end for all sorts of crimes.

"The immediate benefits would be profound and fundamental. Theft of cash would become impossible. Bank robberies and cash-register robberies would simply cease to occur. Attacks on shopkeepers, taxi drivers, and cashiers would all end…Urban streets would become safer…Security costs and insurance rates would fall. Property values would rise…Sales of illegal drugs, along with the concomitant violent crime, should diminish. Hospital emergency rooms would become less crowded…A change from cash to recorded electronic money would be accompanied by a flow of previously unpaid income-tax revenues running in the tens of billions of dollars. As a result, income-tax rates could be lowered or the national debt reduced."[17]

Don't you feel safer already? Oh, but that's not all. Smart cards not only promise to provide a whole new sense of security, but they can even be used in three different ways: the **card itself**, **your computer**, and even your **cell phone**. For instance, **as a card**, you can use it to not only pay for virtually anything at any business, but now with another device called PET, or Personal Electronic Transfer, you can exchange money with other smart card users.[18] So if you owe somebody $20, you still don't need cash in your pocket. Just zap it from your smart card to theirs.

Oh, but that's not all. With **your computer**, you can now use what's called a smart card reader. It's an inexpensive device that looks like a floppy drive that you insert your smart card into. Now you can make purchases on the Internet or even transfer money from your checking account **directly onto the card**. Now you have your own personal ATM machine.[19] In fact, it is expected that soon, computer manufacturers will be installing smart card readers as **standard equipment** on all their machines.[20]

Oh, but just in case you don't have computer access handy, you can also use **your cell phone**. Right now, cell phones are doubling as mobile cash machines to make purchases from street vendors to pizza delivery.[21] And just in case you don't have one of these new phones, no need to fear! Nokia has developed a **"clip-on" smart card reader** for cell phones. And now, with the wave of your phone, you can buy just about anything from a boat to a burger, like this article stated:

"Grabbing a burger is getting easier. Soon you will just have to wave your cell phone as you pass McDonald's drive-through. Immediate gratification is always the best marketing tool.

Nokia is testing a new SmartCover for its… phones that will act just like a debit card…expected to hit the stores before June.

There is no dialing, no ATM, no fumbling for a wallet or dropped coins – only radio-frequency burgers."[22]

Now, as weird as all this new technology sounds, you might still be thinking that this is all nice and dandy, but it's never going to catch on. But folks, **four billion** smart cards were issued in 2000 alone![23] In fact, **right now** in Europe, smart cards are not only commonplace but will soon be a necessity. England is expecting to have all governmental services online and will issue their citizens smart cards in order to access the system.[24]

Oh, but that's not all. **Right now**, here in America, smart cards are being heavily promoted by celebrities like Britney Spears, who's offering her fans five collectable smart card flash cards so they can get access to behind-the-scenes videos or photos on her website.[25] And not to be left out, in light of the terrorist attacks, last year the Pentagon made smart cards **mandatory** for **four million** troops and civilians, in order to open secure doors, get cash, buy food, and check out weapons and military hardware.[26] And that's right, due to promises of eliminating fraud and saving money, banks are also jumping on the bandwagon. **Right now**, MasterCard is planning on turning their six hundred million debit cards into smart cards.[27]

And speaking of MasterCard, they recently purchased fifty-one percent of a smart card company called MONDEX.[28] And MONDEX just happens to be **the only electronic cash system in the world** that allows for multiple currencies on one card.[29] In fact, so excited is MONDEX about this backing from MasterCard, that they have stated, "This is the final stage in becoming a global reality. With MasterCard's backing, there's nothing to stop MONDEX now from becoming the global standard."[30]

Then, as if that wasn't weird enough, the president of Visa has hinted at taking the tiny microchips from their plastic smart cards and putting them into much "handier things" such as a **watch or even a ring**.[31] I mean, come on, what's next? Some sort of smart card tattoo or body implant? Folks, it might be closer than you think. You see, it is said that MONDEX stands for Monetary Dexter. And if you'll look for yourself in the dictionary, you will see that monetary means, **"pertaining to money"** and dexter means **"right hand."** Hey, wait a second. Money in the right hand? Where have we heard that before?

Now I don't know about you guys, but it sure sounds like somebody is taking this **One World Economy** very seriously, how about you? Just like the Bible said. When? In the last days!

And folks, believe it or not, even with all this amazing evidence pointing to the signs of Christ's soon return, some people still need **to have the truth repeated to them over and over again**, like this guy discovered:

"A small guy walks into a diner one day and heads straight for the counter and has a seat on one of the stools. And while he's deciding on what he's going to order, he decides to have a little fun and so leans over to the big woman next to him and says, 'Hey, lady. Do you wanna hear a funny blonde joke?'

Well, immediately the big woman gives him a horrible look and replies, 'Well, before you tell that joke, you should know something mister. I'm blonde, and six feet tall, 210 lbs. and I'm a professional triathlete and bodybuilder.

Not to mention the blonde woman sitting next to me is 6'2" and 220 lbs. and she's an ex-professional wrestler.

And if you'll notice, that waitress over there is also a blonde who's 6'5", weighs 250 lbs. and she's a professional kickboxer.

You see buddy, we're three big, bad blondes! Now, funny guy, do you still want to tell that blonde joke?'

So the guy blinks and swallows, thinks about it a second and says, 'No way! Not if I'm going to have to explain it three times.'"[32]

Now, that guy wasn't about to keep repeating himself over and over again, was he? But do you know what? Neither will God. You see, many people today think that their lives are going to be filled with untold riches and absolute security through **A One World Economy**. They think that they have all the time in the world to respond to the gospel after they first go and make all their riches. But the Bible says that God isn't going to keep repeating His message of salvation over and over again. The offer won't be there forever. He simply says that if you hear His voice calling you, you need to respond today.

Hebrews 3:7-8,10-11 "That is why the Holy Spirit says, 'Today you must listen to his voice. Don't harden your hearts against him as Israel did when they rebelled, when they tested God's patience in the wilderness. There your ancestors tried my patience, even though they saw my miracles for forty years. So I was angry with them, and I said, Their hearts always turn away from me. They refuse to do what I tell them. So in my anger I made a vow: They will never enter my place of rest.'" (NLT)

People of God, I hope you're not one of those who have bought into this lie that man can somehow manifest his own heaven on earth by creating **A One World Economy**. Why? Because you might wake up one day and discover that **you've been left behind**. And do you know what? God doesn't want you left behind. Because He loves you and I, He has given us the warning sign of **A One World Economy** to show us that the Tribulation **could be near** and that Christ's 2nd Coming is rapidly approaching. Jesus Himself said this:

Luke 21:28 "When these things begin to take place, stand up and lift up your heads, because your redemption is drawing near." (NIV)

Like it or not folks, we are headed for **The Final Countdown**. We don't know the day or the hour. Only God knows. The point is, if you're a Christian and you haven't noticed; there are no U-hauls behind a hearse. Therefore, let's stop pampering our lusts and let's start praying for the lost! Folks, it's high time we Christians speak up and declare the good news of salvation to those who are dying all around us. But please, if you're not a Christian, give your life to Jesus today, because tomorrow may be too late! Just like the Bible said!

Study Questions

___

<u>Review</u>

Try to fill in as many as you can on the Final Countdown.

Sign #10 was The _____ _____

Sign # 9 was _____ _____

Sign # 8 was _____ _____

Sign #7 was The _____ _____ _____

Sign #6 was The _____ _____ _____

Sign #5 was The _____ _____ _____

Sign #4 was A _____ _____ _____

Sign #3 was A _____ _____ _____

In the last chapter Pastor Billy shared with us two indicators, in these last days, that our world is headed toward a One World Government. They are:

   ✓ A new world _____

   ✓ A new world _____ system

<u>This Chapter:</u>

The #2 sign of the Final Countdown is none other than A One World

_____, controlled by the antichrist.

Revelation 13:11,12,16,17 "Then I saw another beast come up out of the earth. He exercised all the authority of the first beast. And he required all the earth and those who belong to this world to worship the first beast. He required everyone – great and small, rich and poor, slave and free – to be given a mark on the right hand or on the forehead. And no one could buy or sell anything without that mark."

- Is there any evidence today that we are globally headed toward a One World Economy? Pastor Billy will share with us two indicators.

The first indicator that we know that we are headed for the One World Economy is due to a Universal _____ System; or in other terms, a _____ _____. Right now there are already in place the plans for absolute _____ _____ of the whole world.

Note the following:

✓ A Universal _____ Institution called the International _____ fund. IMF oversees the world's financial system, fixing the exchange rates.

✓ A Universal Money _____ called "SWIFT" the Universal Electronic Banking System. SWIFT makes sure that all the different money transactions match all the different currencies in the world.

✓ A Universal Strong Arm, called the World _____ Organization. The WTO sets the trading rules for the world and punishes all countries who don't obey with billion dollar fines and sanctions.

But guess what? That's not all there is to this economic control of the whole world. These same economic powers have already divided up the world into _____ Economic Kingdoms in order to assure proper control. And by the way, this economic world division is designed by an economic club from _____.

This sounds just like the prophecy we read of in Revelation 17:9, 12-13 where it talks about the coming of a revived Roman Empire with its ten-horned kingdom under the power of the antichrist.

Revelation 17:9,12-13 "And now understand this. His ten horns are ten kings who have not yet risen to power; they will be appointed to their kingdoms for one brief moment to reign with the beast. They will all agree to give their power and authority to him."

- What unified steps are being taken toward this 10-horned economic federation?

Answer:

- ✓ The _____ Union with their own currency called the _____
- ✓ The _____ Union with their own currency called the _____ _____
- ✓ The _____ _____ Union with their own currency called the _____.

Plans are in the making for:

- ✓ A South American Union
- ✓ An Asian Union
- ✓ A Central Asian Union
- ✓ A Pacific Union
- ✓ A Mediterranean Union

The second indicator that we know that we are headed for a One World Economy is due to a Universal _____; or in other terms, the coming _____ Society.

In the last century alone, we have gone from _____ currency to _____ cash. We have come from paper money to writing a _____, to charging it to a _____ card, to taking it out of your checking account with a _____ card. And now all of these features, and much more, are all combined into one magical card called the _____ card.

Some experts are saying that these smart cards "will soon be the world's first truly _____ currency. In this card is a tiny _____ that can store and receive an unlimited amount of information. They can be used for all kinds of things:

1. Personal ATM
2. Purchases (stores, restaurants, vending machines, gas, toll roads, etc.)
3. Telephone calls
4. Access to cable and satellite programs
5. Internet purchases
6. Vehicle and building access
7. Personal computer access (replace all passwords)
8. Loyalty programs (airlines, grocery stores, etc.)
9. Rapid Check-in (hotels, airlines, etc.)
10. Personal Identification Holder (Soc. Security, Driver's License, Student ID, Health and Insurance ID, voting information, picture, and fingerprints)

How convenient that if we got rid of all paper currency, these smart cards would automatically make our world a safer place to live. One person stated:

"The immediate benefits would be profound and fundamental. Theft of cash would become impossible. Bank robberies and cash-register robberies would simply cease to occur. Attacks on shopkeepers, taxi drivers, and cashiers would all end…Urban streets would become safer…Security costs and insurance rates would fall. Property values would rise…Sales of illegal drugs, along with the concomitant violent crime, should diminish. Hospital emergency rooms would become less crowded…A change from cash to recorded electronic money would be accompanied by a flow of previously unpaid income-tax revenues running in the tens of billions of dollars. As a result, income-tax rates could be lowered or the national debt reduced."

These cards can be used in three different ways:

- ✓ The card itself
- ✓ Your computer
- ✓ Your cell phone

- What is expected very soon?

Answer: Computer manufacturers will be installing smart card _____ as _____ equipment on _____ their machines.

- How many smart cards were issued in the year 2000 alone?

Answer: four _____

In 2007 the Pentagon made smart cards _____ for four million troops

and civilians. Right now, _____ is planning on turning their 600

million debit cards into smart cards.

In fact, MasterCard recently purchased 51 percent of a smart card company called _____. MONDEX is the only electronic cash system in the world that allows for multiple currencies on one card.

- What did MONDEX itself state about this backing from MasterCard?

Answer: "This is the final stage in becoming a global reality. With MasterCard's backing, there's nothing to stop MONDEX now from becoming the global standard."

The president of Visa wants to take these tiny microchips in the smart cards and put them into much "handier things" like a _____ or even a

_____.

- Could this sort of thing be placed in a tattoo or body implant?

Answer: Consider what MONDEX stands for – Monetary Dexter:

✓ Monetary = "pertaining to _____"
✓ Dexter = "right hand"

Money in the right hand? Sounds very Biblical and prophetical to me!

The 2 Coming of Jesus Christ is closer than we think. And God has been gracious and merciful to warn us ahead of time. We dare not harden our hearts against God's voice. He is calling you to get right with Him **today**.

Listen: Hebrews 3:7-8,10-11 "That is why the Holy Spirit says, today you must listen to his voice. Don't harden your hearts against him as Israel did when they rebelled, when they tested God's patience in the wilderness. There your ancestors tried my patience, even though they saw my miracles for forty years. So I was angry with them, and I said, their hearts always turn away from me. They refuse to do what I tell them. So in my anger I made a vow: They will never enter my place of rest."

"They will never enter my place of rest."

What a sobering warning to all of us! **Today** is the day to settle things with God. God promises in Romans 10:13, "Whoever calls on the name of the LORD shall be saved."

Make sure **today**!

Chapter Ten

The Mark of the Beast

"A man was sitting at home one evening, when the doorbell rang. And when he answered the door, a 6-foot tall cockroach was standing there. But before the man could do anything, the cockroach immediately punched him between the eyes and scampered off.

Well, the next evening, the man was sitting at home when the doorbell rang again. And when he answered the door, there was the cockroach again. And this time it punched him, kicked him and karate chopped him and then scampered away.

And believe it or not, the third evening came and the man was sitting at home when the doorbell rang. And that's right, when he answered the door the cockroach was there yet again.

This time it leapt at him and stabbed him several times before scampering off. At this the gravely injured man managed to crawl to the telephone and summoned for an ambulance. Soon he was rushed to intensive care, where they were barely able to save his life.

So the next morning, the doctor was doing his rounds and he asked the man what happened. So the man explained about the surprising nightly attacks of the 6-foot cockroach, which culminated in the near fatal stabbing.

But not at all surprised himself, the doctor simply informed the man, 'Yes, there's a nasty bug going around.'"[1]

Now, that doctor wasn't at all surprised about what happened to that man, was he? And it's all because he was well informed about the danger that was out there, right? But unfortunately, many people aren't very well informed about another danger that's out there. And that's the danger of God's wrath, which is one day coming upon this wicked and rebellious planet. And because people refuse to get right with God through Jesus and get saved, they are sadly running the risk of being left behind and will be catapulted into the seven-year Tribulation that is coming upon the whole world.

And folks, the time of the Tribulation is not a party. Jesus said in **Matthew 24** that it would be a time of greater horror than anything the world has ever seen or will ever see again. He also said that unless that time of calamity is shortened, the entire human race would be destroyed. But God is not only a God of wrath. He's a God of love as well. And **because He loves you and I**, He has given us many warning signs so that we would know when the Tribulation could be near and that Christ's 2nd Coming is rapidly approaching. Therefore, to make sure we're not surprised about the dangers of being left behind, we're going to take one last look at **The Final Countdown**.

We already saw how the **#10** sign on **The Final Countdown** was **The Jewish People**. The **#9** sign was **Modern Technology**. The **#8** sign was **Worldwide Upheaval**. The **#7** sign was **The Rise of Falsehood**. The **#6** sign was **The Rise of Wickedness**. The **#5** sign was **The Rise of Apostasy**. The **#4** sign was a **One World Religion**. The **#3** sign was **A One World Government**. In the last chapter we saw how the **#2** sign was none other than **A One World Economy**. There we saw that God lovingly foretold you and I that when we see a worldwide economy of the antichrist that this would be an indicator that we are in the last days. And isn't that what we see **today** with this push for a universal banking system and a universal currency?

But that's not the only signs that God has given us. The **#1** sign on **The Final Countdown** is none other than **The Mark of the Beast**. So just what are these specific prophesies being fulfilled today concerning **The Mark of the Beast**, revealing that we could be in the last days? Well, I'm glad you asked. Let's take a look. The **1st** End Time Prophecy concerning **The Mark of the Beast** is that **there will be a worldwide mark of the antichrist**.

Revelation 13:16-17; 14:9-11 "He required everyone – great and small, rich and poor, slave and free – to be given a mark on the right hand or on the forehead. And no one could buy or sell anything without that mark, which was either the name of the beast or the number representing his name.

Anyone who worships the beast and his statue or who accepts his mark on the forehead or the hand must drink the wine of God's wrath. It is poured out undiluted into God's cup of wrath. And they will be tormented with fire and burning sulfur in the presence of the holy angels and the Lamb. The smoke of their torment rises forever and ever, and they will have no relief day or night, for they have worshiped the beast and his statue and have accepted the mark of his name." (NLT)

According to this passage of Scripture, there is coming a day when all unsaved people of the earth will be deceived into receiving a mark on their bodies, either on the right hand or forehead, that represents the antichrist himself. One day, the whole world of unbelievers will be unified with **The Mark of the Beast** that will actually seal their fate of eternal destruction. But the question is, "Could that really happen? Could the whole world really be deceived into receiving **The Mark of the Beast**? And is there any evidence that this is really going to take place just like the Bible said?" You bet there is! Let's take a look.

The **1ˢᵗ way** we know that people will soon be receiving **The Mark of the Beast** is because **The Technology Is Already Here**. You see, if you're going to deceive people into receiving **The Mark of the Beast** then you've got to have the technology in place to pull it off, right? Well gee, guess what? For the **1ˢᵗ time in mankind's history**, the means to monitor and control every person on the planet is now available. And this is now possible through satellite technology. **Right now**, Motorola has launched 66 low-orbiting satellites that can not only pick up signals from certain types of microchips, but now it's common knowledge that this kind of tracking system was **already used** to monitor the locations of military personnel in the war with Iraq.[2] In fact, this ability to monitor people with satellites is so common that it is currently being used to spy on boat traffic in Florida.[3] Even garbage men in England are being watched from the sky on their jobs on order to make sure that they don't linger too long in one spot.[4] Oh, but that's not all. Thanks to the backing by Bill Gates, we now have what's called **Internet In The Sky**. This is a system of 840 low-altitude satellites in twenty-one orbits with forty satellites in each orbit that creates a virtual electronic blanket around the whole planet. And now you can communicate and monitor any person anywhere on the planet from the top of the Himalayas to the Dead Sea.[5]

But wait a second, if you're going to monitor and control the whole planet with **The Mark of the Beast,** you not only need to track them wherever they go, but you also need some sort of database to identify who they are. Well gee, guess what. **Right now**, these kinds of mega-databases are already available. For instance, a U.S. company called Acxiom operates one of the world's largest databases on ninety-five percent of all American households.[6] Twenty-four hours a day, they gather and store information on you and I from credit card transactions, magazine subscriptions, telephone numbers, real estate records, car registrations, and even fishing licenses, to name a few. And because of all this information, **they can provide a full profile** of each one of us, right down to whether we own a dog or cat, enjoy camping or gourmet cooking, read the Bible or other books, what our occupation is, what car we drive, what videos we watch, how much gas and food we buy, and even where our favorite vacations spots are.[7] In fact, it is estimated that, **right now**, each adult in the developed world is **already located**, on average, in **three hundred different databases**.[8]

But wait a second, if you're going to monitor and control the whole planet with **The Mark of the Beast**, you not only need some sort of database to identify who they are, but you also need some way to personally connect them to this global system, right? Well gee, guess what? **Right now**, especially in light of the terrorist attacks, there has been an explosion of all kinds of personal identification devices. Let's take a look at just a few of them:

1. Intel Corp. is supposed to, or already has, started imbedding identification numbers in its computer processors, which allows everyone to be identified on the Internet.
2. Anyone carrying a cell phone can now be precisely pinpointed.
3. There are currently 1.1 billion facial images already in databases throughout the world.
4. Florida police have linked surveillance cameras to facial recognition software and are using them to instantly recognize and match "wanted people" to image databases.
5. Australian schools are using a watch-like device worn by students to monitor how much exercise the children are getting.
6. Acme rental cars are using GPS systems to monitor rental car users behavior and fines people $150 for each occurrence of excessive speed.
7. Denver city employee vehicles are now being monitored at all times using GPS systems to indicate purpose of the trip, route taken, distance traveled, and the time of the journey.

8. Three police officers were recently charged with falsifying records when their reports didn't match the location indicated by GPS systems installed in their vehicles.
9. Hand and retinal scans are being used by businesses and airports to automatically identify travelers.
10. Fingerprint scans are now being used in America to access computers, buy groceries, and purchase school lunches.[9]

Now as you can see, every single person can accurately and specifically be identified in a variety of ways. In fact, **right now** schools in Belgium are **using all three technologies**, satellites, databases, and personal identification devices, to monitor students. Each student is required to carry a chip-card and all the teacher needs to do to know if a child is late or absent is to log onto this system and instantly they can find out exactly where the missing child is.[10]

However, **there are a few problems** with these kinds of identification systems. They either take too much time, they can be damaged or falsified, or worse yet, they can be lost. So if you're going to monitor and control every person on the planet, then you need some kind of universal tracking and personal identification device **that can't be falsified or lost**, right? Well gee, guess what? It's already been invented. **Right now**, you can get your very own **biometric implant**. What's that? Well, in case you haven't already heard, a biometric implant is a tiny little chip about the size of a grain of rice that is implanted just beneath the skin. Its benefits are that it can't be stolen and you can't lose it, for it's with you wherever you go. And folks, you must understand that this isn't some science fiction fantasy that might take place centuries from now. **It's already here**! In case you haven't already heard, a **new implant device** called the **Digital Angel** has the ability to not only pinpoint a person's location but it can even monitor vital signs like the heart rate or blood pressure.[11] The only thing that was holding it up was governmental approval. But you'll be happy to know,

as you saw two chapters ago, that **it was approved by the FDA in 2002**.[12] Now,
correct me if I'm wrong, but I'd say somebody's very serious about
implementing **The Mark of the Beast**, how about you? Just like the Bible said.
When? In the last days.

The **2nd way** we know that people will soon be receiving **The Mark of
the Beast** is because **The Justification Is Already Here**. You see, if you're
going to deceive people into receiving **The Mark of the Beast**, then you've got
to have people convinced that this would actually be a good thing to do, right?
Well gee, guess what? For the **1st time in mankind's history**, people have been
prepped to think that the total control over all areas of their lives via microchips
is the greatest thing that could ever happen. How's that? Well, I'm glad you
asked. The **1st way** that people are being prepped for an invasion of microchip
control is that **they promise to make our lives more pampered**. How can they
do that? Well, let's take a look at just a few of the examples out there:

1. You can have tiny cell phones implanted into your bikinis.
2. You can have T-shirts implanted with Internet links.
3. You can have baby nappies or tennis shoes implanted with tracking devices.
4. You can have implanted jackets to wear that allow you to switch on the TV,
   check phone messages, or even tell the oven to start cooking a meal.
5. You can have implants in your house to customize anything from the
   temperature to even background music.
6. You can have implants in your car to access the Internet or pay for toll
   charges, gas, or even food in a Drive Thru.
7. You can have implants in television sets that eject artificial scents when
   different advertisements or scenes are viewed. (I told you watching TV
   smells!)
8. You can have implants that sense brain wave patterns and converts them into
   signals used to operate electrical appliances.
9. You can have implants that act like "intelligent shopping agents" who will
   know everything about you from personal quirks to shoe size and will search
   instantly anywhere in the world via the Internet to find you the best deal.

10. You can have an implant in your fingertip that will transfer all your vital personal information with a handshake. (A digital authentication law has already been passed through Congress giving these "electronic signatures" the same legal status as writing your name on a document.)[13]

Now, who wouldn't want their lives filled with such creature comforts, huh? I mean, come on, wouldn't it be **cool** to have a microchip implant? Folks, that's precisely the selling point. In fact, two articles went on to say this:

"How'd you like to avoid waiting in lines for the rest of your life? Breeze through everywhere like you owned the place. Watch lights snap on, doors open automatically, money pop out of ATMs as you approach. Never have to show an ID, buy a ticket, carry keys, remember a password. You'd leave stores loaded with packages and waltz right past the cashiers. You wouldn't have to carry a wallet. Ever. Family and friends could find you instantly in any crowd."

"These latest injectable devices have taken things a step further. What next? I approach my car, which knows who I am. The door swings open and the driver seat and steering wheel adjust to my usual settings, the radio starts to play my favorite station and a speech unit offers to navigate me to Heathrow. As I board the plane, a sensor in the aircraft door activates the chip which tells the on-board flight system who I am. 'Welcome…seat 4a is ready for you. This flight is worth 450 air-miles.' I arrive in New York and hire a car, which also recognizes me and adjusts accordingly. The hotel room unlocks and bills me as I enter. Room service arrives to stock the fridge with favorite…items plus the extras I usually order. None of this is science fiction. All of this is possible using today's tools. It is just a question of connecting them together."[14]

Now I don't know about you guys, but I think we're being prepped for an invasion of implants because, after all, **they'll make our lives so much more pampered**. And isn't that what everybody wants?

The **2nd way** people are being prepped for an invasion of microchip control is that **they promise to make our lives more productive**. How can they do that? Well, let's take a look at just a few of the examples out there:

1. You can have tiny implants on all manufactured items to create a self-managing intelligent supply chain that will track all products from the factory, to the home, to the recycling center.
2. You can have tiny implants on all luggage and packages to ensure their exact whereabouts.
3. You can have implants for your employees to monitor their location, who their with, their timekeeping, efficiency and productivity.
4. You can have another implant for your restaurant employees so that when they use the restroom it activates another implant in the washbasin to monitor whether or not they washed their hands and alert you if there's a need for disciplinary action.
5. You can have an implant to act as an internal alarm clock that determines how much sleep you can get.
6. You can have an implant to constantly monitor your body functions such as pulse, heart rate, sugar levels, etc.
7. You can have an implant to connect you directly to your computer.
8. You can have an implant to send an electrode to your brain to send another electrode to a former paralyzed muscle or limb.
9. You can have an implant connected to the eye to provide sight for the blind.
10. You can have an implant to extend human intelligence or memory.[15]

Now, who doesn't need one of those memory implants, huh? I mean, come on, wouldn't it be **constructive** to have a microchip implant? Folks, that's precisely the selling point. And I don't know about you guys, but I think we're being prepped for an invasion of implants because, after all, **they'll make our lives so much more productive**. And isn't that what everybody wants?

The **3rd way** people are being prepped for an invasion of microchip control is that **they promise to make our lives more protected**. How can they do that? Well, let's take a look at just a few of the examples out there:

1. You can have an implant in your pet to make sure it never gets lost.
2. You can have an implant in your car that will automatically alert police when it's stolen and pinpoint it's exact location.
3. You can have an implant to instantly find people involved in airplane crashes or other natural disasters.

4. You can have an implant to instantly alert you if someone's body temperature has changed like from falling in water or in a fire.
5. You can have an implant put on nuclear devices, machines, or dams to give advance notice of impending danger.
6. You can have an implant put in businesses to instantly alert you of break-ins or tampering.
7. You can have an implant to monitor and pinpoint missing livestock.
8. You can have an implant to automatically monitor parolees and save money on prison costs.
9. You can have an implant to find out if an Alzheimer patient has wandered off.
10. You can have an implant to instantly locate a lost or abducted child.[16]

Now, who wouldn't want to have their property or loved ones protected at all times, huh? I mean come on, wouldn't it be **common sense** to have a microchip implant? That's precisely the selling point. In fact, in light of the terrorist attacks and all the media coverage on child abductions lately, it seems just about everybody is hopping on the bandwagon. See for yourself:

- **Rep. Mary Bono** said some of our freedoms will have to be surrendered for the sake of security.

- **Digital Angel Spokesman** said, "We've changed our thinking since September 11. Now there's more of a need to monitor evil activities."

- **Dr. Peter Zhou** chief scientist of Digital Angel said, "A few years ago there may have been resistance, but not anymore. People are getting used to having implants. New century, new trend...this will be very, very popular. Fifty years ago the thought of a cell phone, where you could walk around talking on the phone, was unimaginable. Now they are everywhere." Just like the cell phone, Digital Angel "will be a connection from yourself to the electronic world. It will be your guardian, protector. It will bring good things to you. We will be a hybrid of electronic intelligence and our own soul."

- **Andy Rooney** said on 60 Minutes, "We need some system for permanently identifying safe people. Most of us are never going to blow anything up and there's got to be something better than one of these photo Ids...I wouldn't mind having something planted permanently in my arm that would identify me."

- **John Walsh of America's Most Wanted** said about implants, "It's a brilliant idea. I wish someone would develop it because, number one, time is crucial when a child is missing and you could locate them by the chip. And even if you weren't lucky enough to locate them, finding the body is crucial for two things: the ending of the search of the parents and helping with the prosecution of the case. So I hope that somebody develops that in my lifetime."

- **Scott Silverman** President of Digital Angel said, "It's a shame that recent tragedies seem to have prompted this increased attention, but the only way to assist in the prevention of future tragedies is for parents, law enforcement and others to become aware of available technologies. Although our technologies have a variety of other applications, we believe VeriChip, Digital Angel and the forthcoming PLD have the potential to help safeguard children and provide greater peace-of-mind to parents"

- **Scott McNealy CEO of Sun Microsystems** foretold of a time when "They're going to slap that baby's bottom, then slip an ID chip in their neck or between their shoulders so you can keep track of your kid."

- **Roger Ebert** echoed "Sometime in the next century, because computer chips are getting smaller and faster, that eventually the time will come when a child is implanted with a little chip back here (in the back of the neck) and will learn to control the chip in the same way that you learn to control your bodily functions and your voice and your movements."[17]

Now, I don't know about you guys, but I think we're being prepped for an invasion of implants because, after all, **they'll make our lives so much more protected**. And isn't that what everybody wants? Correct me if I'm wrong, but I'd say somebody's very serious about implementing **The Mark of the Beast**, how about you? Just like the Bible said. When? In the last days.

The **3rd way** we know that people will soon be receiving **The Mark of the Beast** is because **The Willingness Is Already Here**. You see, if you're going to deceive people into receiving **The Mark of the Beast**, then you've got to have people prepped to give it a try, right? Well gee, guess what? For the **1ˢᵗ time in mankind's history**, people have already been prepped to receive microchip implants. How's that? Well, I'm glad you asked. The **1ˢᵗ way** that people have been prepped to receive a microchip implant is that **they've already put them into pets**. In fact, putting microchips into pets is not only commonplace, but now they're becoming mandatory. At first, they were voluntary through animal implant companies like INFOPET to keep track of stray animals. However, that was soon to change. **Right now**, in many places across our country, it's **mandatory** to have your pet microchipped or you can't get them out of the pound. In fact, Israel has recently become the first nation to require **all their pets** to be given an implant.[18]

I mean, come on, what's next people? Well, it's funny you should mention that. You see, the **2ⁿᵈ way** people have been prepped to receive a microchip implant is that **they've already put them into people**. At first, it was special dignitaries whose position put them in jeopardy of being kidnapped. However, that was soon to change. In 1996 we saw Professor Kevin Warwick experiment by putting a chip in his arm. Why? He thought it would be cool to be able to automatically unlock doors, turn on lights, and boot up his computer as soon as he walked into the room. In fact, after the experiment was over, Warwick had this to say:

"'After a few days I started to feel quite a closeness to the computer, which was very strange,' he muses. 'When you are linking your brain up like that, you change who you are. You do become a 'borg.' You are not just a human linked with technology; you are something different and your values and judgment will change.'"[19]

Now admittedly, his wife thought Kevin was a bit weird and wanted nothing to do with his implant experiment. And you might also be tempted to think that no normal person would ever willingly go along with an implant. But in light of the terrorist attacks, the recent rise of child abductions, and FDA approval for Digital Angel, **for the 1st time in mankind's history**, people are lining up to receive a microchip implant. One such family is the Jacobs family from Florida. They willingly had their whole family implanted with microchips. Where? In their right arms.[20] Hmmm. That's not too far away from the right hand is it? In fact, they're not the only ones. Now that the floodgates are opened, thousands of kids and adults are expressing their willing interest in being microchipped too.[21] And boy, the propaganda machines are just now gearing up to ensure that implants soon become as natural as hot dogs and apple pie. One article said this:

"Worry no more, doting parents! Whether it's your little pumpkin's first day walking home from school by herself or the millionth time you've lost her at the mall, the Babysitter™ will track your sweetpea's location from a jelly bean-sized microchip implant, discreetly tucked under her collarbone.

Also available: The Constant Companion™ lets you keep a watchful eye on grandma or grandpa, even when you can't be by their side. Coming soon: The INS Border Patroller™; the Personal Private Eye™; the Micro-Manager™. Alas, this is not as far-fetched or as futuristic as it sounds. The notion of surveillance chips being installed in human beings is poised to cross over from the realm of science fiction into everyday reality, and soon."[22]

Oh, but that's still not all. If you do the homework, you'll se that these propaganda machines have actually been in place for a long time now as this article shares.

"As far back as 1973, Senior Scholastics introduced school age children to the concept of buying and selling using numbers inserted in their forehead. In the September 20, 1973 feature 'Who Is Watching You?' the secular high school journal speculated: 'All buying and selling in the program will be done by computer. No currency, no change, no checks. In the program, people would receive a number that had been assigned them tattooed in their wrist or forehead. The number is put on by laser beam and cannot be felt. The number in the body is not seen with the naked eye and is as permanent as your fingerprints. All items of consumer goods will be marked with a computer mark. The computer outlet in the store which picks up the number on the items at the checkstand will also pick up the number in the person's body and automatically total the price and deduct the amount from the person's 'Special Drawing Rights' account.'

In the 1974 article 'The Specter of Eugenics,' Charles Frankel pointed out Linus Pauling's (Nobel Prize winner) suggestions that a mark be tattooed on the foot or forehead of every young person. Pauling envisioned a mark denoting genotype.

In 1980, U.S. News and World Report continued the warning, pointing out that the Federal Government was contemplating 'National Identity Cards,' without which nobody could work or conduct business.

The Denver Post Sun followed up in 1981, claiming that chip implants could someday replace I.D. cards. The June 21, 1981 story read in part, 'The chip is placed in a needle which is affixed to a simple syringe containing an anti-bacterial solution. The needle is capped and ready to forever identify something – or somebody.'

The May 7, 1996 Chicago Tribune questioned the technology, wondering aloud if we could trust Big Brother under our skin?

Then in 1997 applications for patents of subcutaneous implant devices for 'a person or an animal' were applied for.

On April 27, 1998, Time Magazine ran the story, The Big Bank Theory And What It Says About The Future OF Money, in which they opined 'Your daughter can store the money any way she wants--on her laptop, on a debit card, even (in the not too distant future) on a chip implanted under her skin.'

In August 1998 the BBC covered the first known human microchip implantation.

That same month the Sunday Portland Oregonian warned that proposed medical identifiers might erode privacy rights by tracking individuals through alphanumeric health identifier technologies. The startling Oregonian feature depicted humans with barcodes in their foreheads.

And recently the Madras High School in the little town of Madras, Oregon is the latest government institution to allow students to pay for their lunch with the swipe of a hand.

Makers of implantable microchips claim the procedure will continue to be voluntary. But a report written by Elaine M. Ramish for the Franklin Pierce Law Center says: 'A [mandatory] national identification system via microchip implants could be achieved in two stages: Upon introduction as a voluntary system, the microchip implantation will appear to be palatable. After there is a familiarity with the procedure and a knowledge of its benefits, implantation would be mandatory.'

George Getz, the communications director for the Libertarian Party agrees, saying: 'After all, the government has never forced anyone to have a driver license, [but] try getting along without one, when everyone from your local banker to the car rental man to the hotel operator to the grocery store requires one in order for you to take advantage of their services, that amounts to a de facto mandate. If the government can force you to surrender your fingerprints to get a drivers license, why can't it force you to get a computer chip implant?'

In the same way Social Security numbers were voluntary before becoming mandatory, biometric chip implants will be compulsory in the future unless citizens take immediate and national opposition. Even Applied Digital Solution's chief executive officer Richard Sullivan envisions a scenario where people [are] required to be chipped or [have] some combination of a device requiring them to be scanned and monitored at all times."[23]

So the question is, "Are the propaganda machines really working?" Well, you tell me. A recent MSNBC poll showed that **right now** 20% of the American population is fully ready and **willing** to receive a microchip implant.[24] And apparently that's why Scott Silverman, the president of Digital Angel is saying that, "he expects that in the next two to three years, it will be standard protocol for emergency room personnel to scan the upper right arm of every patient admitted."[25]

I mean, come on, what's next, some orchestrated plan to put it all into place? Well, it's funny you should mention that. You see, the **3rd way** that people have been prepped to receive a microchip implant is that **they've already put them into their plans**. You see, what most people don't realize is that even if you refuse to receive a body implant now, as was eluded above, you might soon have too. And maybe that's why Senator Joseph Biden said this to Judge John Roberts during his hearing just prior to his becoming America's Chief Justice of the Supreme Court.

"And we will be faced with equally consequential decisions in the 21st century. Can a microscopic tag be implanted in a person's body to track his every movement? There's actual discussion about that. You will rule on that, mark my words, before your tenure is over. Can brain scans be used to determine whether a person is inclined toward criminality or violent behavior? You will rule on that."[26]

But you might object, "Hey that can't happen! Surely it would be against the law." Well, actually, it already is the law. It only needs to be implemented. For instance, as of 1986, with the passage of the Immigration Control Act, this now "gives the President the authority to implement whatever type of identification is necessary to control the population."[27] And if people don't want to go along with this, then all that needs to happen is another national crisis or emergency, and **by law** the President can put it into action, through the Federal Emergency Management Agency, or FEMA, special executive orders to "restore order." What special executive orders? Well, here are just a few:

- Executive Order #10995 - Seizure of all communications media in the United States.
- Executive Order #10997 - Seizure of all electric power, fuels, and minerals, both public and private.

- Executive Order #10998 - Seizure of all food supplies and resources, public, and private, all farms and farm equipment.
- Executive Order #10999 - Seizure of all means of transportation, including personal cars, trucks or vehicles of any kind and total control over all highways, seaports and waterways.
- Executive Order #11000 - Seizure of all American population for work forces under federal supervision, including dividing families as necessary according to governmental plans.
- Executive Order #11001 - Seizure of all health, education and welfare facilities, both public and private.
- Executive Order #11002 - Empowers the Postmaster General to register all men, women and children in the U.S.
- Executive Order #11003 - Seizure of all airports and aircraft.
- Executive Order #11004 - Seizure of all housing and finance authorities, to establish Forced Relocation. Designates areas to be abandoned as "unsafe," establishes new locations for populations, relocates communications, builds new housing with public ('tax-payers') funds.
- Executive Order #11005 - Seizure of all railroads, inland waterways and storage facilities, public and private.
- Executive Order #11051 - Provides the Office of Emergency Planning complete authorization to put the above orders into effect in times of increased international tension or economic or financial crisis.
- Executive Order #11490 - Combines Executive Orders #11001 to #11005 and #11051 into a single Executive Order.
- Executive Order #11921 - F.E.M.A. is authorized to develop plans to control energy, prices and wages, credit and the money supply to U.S. banks in the event of a 'National Emergency.' Congress may not review a President's decision to enforce a 'National Emergency' for six months.
- Executive Order #12656 - The National Security Council given authority to determine requisite emergency powers (increased domestic surveillance, isolation of communities, restriction of movement for groups and individuals in the USA, control of airspace, use of the national guard to enforce laws and seal borders).
- Executive Order #12919 - Signed June 3, 1994, by President Clinton. "National Defense Industrial Resources Preparedness" delegates authorities, responsibilities and allocations of F.E.M.A.'s Executive Orders for the confiscation of ALL PROPERTY from the American people, and their re-location and assignment to 'labor' camps. This Executive Order also supersedes or revokes eleven (11) previous Executive Orders [from 1939

through 1991] and amends Executive Order #10789 and #11790. The declaration of a 'National Emergency' by the President may immediately lead to the implementation of all or part of these provisions and if he so desires he may implement martial law, suspend the Constitution, nullify habeas corpus and all other personal liberties and rights.[28]

Now, did you notice the order there for the Post Office to "register" all men, women, and children? Hmmm. I wonder what they will use to register everyone with?

But you might still object saying, "There's no way a government would ever require people to receive a universal identification mark." Well, not only did Hitler do it with the Jews, but even more recently the European Union is preparing to give its citizens a universal identification so they can "freely move about from country to country."[29] In fact, Japan "launched a compulsory ID system" called Juki Net that links all citizens to a nationwide computer system.[30] And lest you think this won't go global just like the Bible said, the United Nations has already outlined a scheme so that "every person in the world" would be "registered under a universal identification."[31] Now, correct me if I'm wrong, but I'd say somebody's very serious about implementing **The Mark of the Beast**, how about you? Just like the Bible said. When? In the last days.

And folks, what's really interesting is that these microchip implants have a unique power source that recharges itself by converting electricity from the fluctuations of the person's body temperature. Furthermore, it just so happens that Dr. Carl Sanders, who worked for thirty-two years designing microchips in the Bio-Med field, said that "Over one and a half million dollars was spent finding out the two places in the body that temperature changes most rapidly."[32] And just where might these best locations in the body be? That's right, **in the forehead** right below the hairline and **the back of the hand**. Hey, that makes sense. That's how you check a child's temperature the old-fashioned way. He then went on to say that there was one drawback with this system. That is, if the chip broke down, the person would get a boil or grievous sore. Now, I don't know about you guys, but that sure sounds a whole lot like what the Bible says is going to happen. To who? To the people who receive **The Mark of the Beast!**

Revelation 16:2 "So the first angel left the Temple and poured out his bowl over the earth, and horrible, malignant sores broke out on everyone who had the mark of the beast and who worshiped his statue." (NLT)

Now folks, believe it or not, even with all this amazing evidence pointing to the signs of Christ's soon return, some people still have a problem recognizing what's going on, like this lady:

"One day a blonde lady had finally had enough. She was tired of everyone assuming that she wasn't very smart just because of hair color. So she decided to do something about it. She went to the hairdresser and had her hair dyed brown.

And as she walked out of the beauty salon, she was feeling quite proud of her new look so she decided to go for a drive in the country. Well after she drove for awhile she suddenly came upon a shepherd.

And she thought this was a perfect opportunity to test out her new look and demonstrate her intelligence. So she walked over to the shepherd and asked, 'If I can guess how many sheep you have, can I take one for a reward?'

Well, the shepherd thought for sure that this lady could never guess the exact number of sheep he had, so he took her bet and let her try. But to his surprise, amazingly she guessed 98, the exact number of sheep he owned.

So feeling rather good about herself, the lady picks up her reward and starts walking back to her car. But before she got to the car, the shepherd tapped her on the shoulder and said, 'Hey lady, if I can guess your natural hair color, can I have my dog back?'"[33]

Now, that lady had a problem recognizing things, didn't she? But unfortunately, she's not alone. Many people today also have a problem recognizing what's really taking place in current events. They have no clue that the rapture of the Church could happen at any time, and that the antichrist's wicked kingdom is being formed right before their very eyes. And the warning that Jesus gave long ago still holds true today.

Luke 12:54-56 "Then Jesus turned to the crowd and said, 'When you see clouds beginning to form in the west, you say, Here comes a shower.' And you are right. When the south wind blows, you say, Today will be a scorcher. And it is. You hypocrites! You know how to interpret the appearance of the earth and the sky, but you can't interpret these present times.'" (NLT)

People of God, I hope you're not one of those who have bought into this lie that man can somehow have his own heaven on earth by implementing **The Mark of the Beast**. Why? Because you might wake up one day and discover that **you've been left behind**. And do you know what? God doesn't want you left behind. Because He loves you and I, He has given us the warning sign of **The Mark of the Beast** to show us that the Tribulation could be near and that Christ's 2nd Coming is rapidly approaching. Jesus Himself said this:

Luke 21:28 "When these things begin to take place, stand up and lift up your heads, because your redemption is drawing near." (NIV)

Like it or not folks, we are headed for **The Final Countdown**. We don't know the day or the hour. Only God knows. The point is, if you're a Christian, "You must never forget the warning recorded for posterity by Martin Niemoeller, the Lutheran minister who lived in Hitler's Germany during the 1930s and 1940s. His words echo down to us over succeeding decades: '**In Germany they came first for the Communists, and I didn't speak up because I wasn't a Communist. Then they came for the Jews, and I didn't speak up because I wasn't a Jew. Then they came for the trade unionists, and I didn't speak up because I wasn't a trade unionist. Then they came for the Catholics, and I**

didn't speak up because I was a Protestant. Then they came for me, and by that time no one was left to speak up.'"[34] Folks, it's high time we Christians speak up and declare the good news of salvation to those who are dying all around us. But please, if you're not a Christian, give your life to Jesus today, because tomorrow may be too late! Just like the Bible said!

Study Questions

Review

How's your total recall? Try to match the sign with its number.

Worldwide Upheaval	Sign # _____
A One World Economy	Sign # _____
The Rise of Wickedness	Sign # _____
A One World Religion	Sign # _____
Modern Technology	Sign # _____
A One World Government	Sign # _____
The Rise of Apostasy	Sign # _____
The Rise of Falsehood	Sign # _____
The Jewish People	Sign # _____

This Chapter:

The #1 Sign on the Final Countdown is none other than the _____ of the

_____ , which will be a _____ mark of the antichrist.

Revelation 13:16-17; 14:9-11 "He required everyone – great and small, rich and poor, slave and free – to be given a mark on the right hand or on the forehead. And no one could buy or sell anything without that mark, which was either the name of the beast or the number representing his name. Anyone who worships the beast and his statue or who accepts his mark on the forehead or the hand must drink the wine of God's wrath. It is poured out undiluted into God's cup of wrath. And they will be tormented with fire and burning sulfur in the presence of the holy angels and the Lamb. The smoke of their torment rises forever and ever, and they will have no relief day or night, for they have worshiped the beast and his statue and have accepted the mark of his name."

According to this passage of Scripture, there is coming a day when all

_____ people of the earth will be deceived into receiving a mark

on their bodies, either on the _____ hand or _____ ..."

THE 1ST WAY

The first way we know that people will soon be receiving the Mark of the Beast is because the _____ is already here. For the first time in mankind's history, people have been prepped to think that the total control over all areas of their lives via microchips is the greatest thing that could ever happen.

The first way that people are being prepped for microchip control is that they promise to make our lives more _____.

1. You can have tiny cell phones implanted into your bikinis.

2. You can have T-shirts implanted with Internet links.

3. You can have baby nappies or tennis shoes implanted with tracking devices.

4. You can have implanted jackets to wear that allow you to switch on the TV, check phone messages, or even tell the oven to start cooking a meal.

5. You can have implants in your house to customize anything from the temperature to even background music.

6. You can have implants in your car to access the Internet or pay for toll charges, gas, or even food in a Drive Thru.

7. You can have implants in television sets that eject artificial scents when different advertisements or scenes are viewed. (I told you watching TV smells!)

8. You can have implants that sense brain wave patterns and converts them into signals used to operate electrical appliances.

9. You can have implants that act like "intelligent shopping agents" who will know everything about you from personal quirks to shoe size and will search instantly anywhere in the world via the Internet to find you the best deal.

10. You can have an implant in your fingertip that will transfer all your vital personal information with a handshake. (A digital authentication law has already been passed through Congress giving these "electronic signatures" the same legal status as writing your name on a document.)

✓ The selling point – "wouldn't it be _____ to have a microchip implant?"

THE 2ᴺᴰ WAY

The second way that people are being prepped for microchip control is that they promise to make our lives more _____ .

1. You can have tiny implants on all manufactured items to create a self-managing intelligent supply chain that will track all products from the factory, to the home, to the recycling center.

2. You can have tiny implants on all luggage and packages to ensure their exact whereabouts.

3. You can have implants for your employees to monitor their location, who they're with, their timekeeping, efficiency and productivity.

4. You can have another implant for your restaurant employees so that when they use the restroom it activates another implant in the washbasin to monitor whether or not they washed their hands and alert you if there's a need for disciplinary action.

5. You can have an implant to act as an internal alarm clock that determines how much sleep you can get.

6. You can have an implant to constantly monitor your body functions such as pulse, heart rate, sugar levels, etc.

7. You can have an implant to connect you directly to your computer.

8. You can have an implant to send an electrode to your brain to send another electrode to a former paralyzed muscle or limb.

9. You can have an implant connected to the eye to provide sight for the blind.

10. You can have an implant to extend human intelligence or memory.

✓ The selling point – "Wouldn't it be _____ to have a microchip implant?"

We know that people will soon be receiving the Mark of the Beast because the _____ is already here. One such family is the Jacob's family from Florida. They willingly had their _____ family implanted with microchips. Where? In their _____ arms. Not too far away from the _____ hand, is it?

Most people don't realize that even if you refuse to receive a body implant now…you might soon have to accept it. Check out what Senator Bidden said to Judge John Roberts:

"And we will be faced with equally consequential decisions in the 21st century. Can a microscopic tag be implanted in a person's body to track his every movement? There's actual discussion about that. You will rule on that, mark my words, before your tenure is over. Can brain scans be used to determine whether a person is inclined toward criminality or violent behavior? You will rule on that."

And folks, what's really interesting is that these microchip implants have a unique power source that recharges itself by converting electricity from the fluctuations of the person's body temperature.

Furthermore, it just so happens that one researcher, who worked for thirty-two years designing microchips in the Bio-Med field, said that:

"Over one and a half million dollars was spent finding out the two places in the body that temperature changes most rapidly."

And just where might these best locations in the body be? That's right, **in the forehead** right below the hairline and **the back of the hand**. Hey, that makes sense. That's how you check a child's temperature the old-fashioned way.

THE 3RD WAY

The third way people are being prepped for microchip control is they promise to make our lives more _____.

1. You can have an implant in your pet to make sure it never gets lost.

2. You can have an implant in your car that will automatically alert police when it's stolen and pinpoint its exact location.

3. You can have an implant to instantly find people involved in airplane crashes or other natural disasters.

4. You can have an implant to instantly alert you if someone's body temperature has changed like from falling in water or in a fire.

5. You can have an implant put on nuclear devices, machines, or dams to give advance notice of impending danger.

6. You can have an implant put in businesses to instantly alert you of break-ins or tampering.

7. You can have an implant to monitor and pinpoint missing livestock.

8. You can have an implant to automatically monitor parolees and save money on prison costs.

9. You can have an implant to find out if an Alzheimer patient has wandered off.

10. You can have an implant to instantly locate a lost or abducted child.

✓ The selling point – "wouldn't it be _____

_____ to have a microchip implant"? In fact, in light of the terrorist attacks and all the media coverage on child abductions lately, it seems just about everybody is hopping on the bandwagon.

- **Dr. Peter Zhou** chief scientist of Digital Angel said, "A few years ago there may have been resistance, but not anymore. People are getting used to having implants. New century, new trend…this will be very, very popular. Fifty years ago the thought of a cell phone, where you could walk around talking on the phone, was unimaginable. Now they are everywhere." Just like the cell phone, Digital Angel "will be a connection from yourself to the electronic world. It will be your guardian, protector. It will bring good things to you. We will be a hybrid of electronic intelligence and our own soul."

- **Andy Rooney** said on 60 Minutes, "We need some system for permanently identifying safe people. Most of us are never going to blow anything up and there's got to be something better than one of these photo IDs…I wouldn't mind having something planted permanently in my arm that would identify me."

- **John Walsh** of America's Most Wanted said about implants, "It's a brilliant idea. I wish someone would develop it because, number one, time is crucial when a child is missing and you could locate them by the chip. And even if you weren't lucky enough to locate them, finding the body is crucial for two things: the ending of the search of the parents and helping with the prosecution of the case. So I hope that somebody develops that in my lifetime."

- **Scott McNealy** CEO of Sun Microsystems foretold of a time when "They're going to slap that baby's bottom, then slip an ID chip in their neck or between their shoulders so you can keep track of your kid."

- **Roger Ebert** echoed "Sometime in the next century, because computer chips are getting smaller and faster, that eventually the time will come when a child is implanted with a little chip back here (in the back of the neck) and will learn to control the chip in the same way that you learn to control your bodily functions, your voice and your movements."

Pastor Billy's book on the Final Countdown is a wake up call to everyone, Christian and non-Christian alike.

These 10-signs have helped us to interpret our present times in light of biblical prophecy. There's no doubt about it – we are living in the last days.

The signs are overwhelming that Jesus Christ is soon, very soon, coming back to gather His people to Himself and then vent His fiery wrath upon an ungodly world.

Remember what Jesus said in Luke 21:28: "When these things begin to take place, stand up and lift up your heads, because your redemption is drawing near."

Make sure **today** that you are one of God's children.

How to Receive Jesus Christ:

1. Admit your need (I am a sinner).

2. Be willing to turn from your sins (repent).

3. Believe that Jesus Christ died for you on the Cross and rose from the grave.

4. Through prayer, invite Jesus Christ to come in and control your life through the Holy Spirit. (Receive Him as Lord and Savior.)

What to pray:

Dear Lord Jesus,

I know that I am a sinner and need Your forgiveness. I believe that You died for my sins. I want to turn from my sins. I now invite You to come into my heart and life. I want to trust and follow You as Lord and Savior.

In Jesus' name. Amen.

Answer Key

Chapter 1 *The Jewish People*

your
family
has
disappeared
missing
left
behind
God's
Wrath
Warning
signs
Ten
The
Jewish
People
return
returned
to
Israel
Nation
May 14, 1948
recaptured
Jerusalem
brought

forth
May 14, 1948
united
nation
926
2,900
currency
shekel
June of 1980
blossom
rose
barren
wasteland
trees
400
million
abundance
flowers
powerful
military
Egypt
Syria
Jordan
Iraq

Lebanon
fifty
center
conflict
oil
reserves
in
Jerusalem
rebuild
temple
north
south
training
new
temple
red
heifer
Artificially
engineering
cloning
building
Mashiach (Messiah)
Luke 21:28 (write-out)

Chapter 2 *Modern Technology*

The
Jewish
People
Modern
Technology
travel
horseback
car
14,000
400
8,300
6
171
5
six-story

eighty
Teleportation
God
arrogant
overconfident
increase
of
knowledge
13-proofs (own
words)
television
internet
unrest
confused
ignorant

violent
ten
Suicide
Serial killers
rushed
frantic
human
era
motion
memory
insanity
Being
Under
Satan's
Yoke

Chapter 3 *Worldwide Upheaval*

The
Jewish
People
Modern
Technology
Worldwide
Upheaval
Increase
of earthquakes
great
13
51
86
over 100
454
1,100
billions
thousands
hundreds of

thousands
fatalities
million
increase
of
famines
under-fed
starving
to
death
100
4
war
embargoes
government
corruption
economic debt
Overzealous
environmentalists

Increase
of
Pestilence
ballistic
36
Tuberculosis
malaria
cholera
diphtheria
black
plague
experimentation
warfare
overuse
antibiotics
mutating
resistant
Increase
of

Wars
universal
150
29
71

200
China
a
nuclear
holocaust

biological
six
The
Truth
Lot's

Chapter 4 *The Rise of Falsehood*

The
Jewish
People
Modern
Technology
Worldwide
Upheaval
earhquakes
famines
pestilence
wars
The
Rise
of
Falsehood
False
Christs
Sun
Myung
Moon
Messia
Lord
Universe
follow
me
Jesus
Siberia
reincarnated
What's

Yours
Name
Lord
Maitreya
healing
springs
weeping
bleeding
divine
fruit
vegetables
10,000
Jose
Luis
de
Miranda
sin
hell
good
symbol
delusions
Jesus Christ
antichrist
deceive
lawlessness
doomed
destruction
God
False

Teachers
false
teachers
destructive
evil
teaching
Mormonism
Christian Science
Charismatic
New
Age
Movement
occult
Satanism
One
World
Religion
Sun Myung Moon
Healthy
earth
sacred
destruction
earth-centered
global
save
worship
god
cleansing
relationship

Purification
cleanse
restore
illness
wicked
good
Healthy
Body
occultic
eating
animals
unify
save
animals
restriction

before
worship
God
plant
based
vegetarianism
diseases
environmentalists
vegetarians
animal
rights
healthier
happier
Heavenly
Host

Angels
UFO
demonic
deception
promote
debunk
spiritual
16,000 mph
inner
space
dimension
spirit
rapture
lying
demons

Chapter 5 *The Rise of Wickedness*

The
Jewish
People
Modern
Technology
Worldwide
Upheaval
Rise
of
Falsehood
False
Christs
False
Teachers
Rise
Wickedness
Love
Themselves
God

love
of
self
love
God
Wicked
Worldview
Humanism
Man
God
Bible
prayer
Ten
Commandments
1960's
Humanism
Oreses Brownson
Christianity
Science

Horace Mann
public
school
replaced
John Dewey
no
absolutes
ally
every
humanism
elimination
superstition
kill
secular
antidote
following
satan
Wicked Worship
self-love

self-esteem
Maslow
Rogers
Ignoring
Refraining
Blaming
Avoiding
Responsibility
Damage
First
Second
God
your
neighbor
love
yourself

self
God
not
forgiven
accepted
loved
less
last
self-deluded
Wicked
Witchcraft
Wicca
Environmentalism
Feminism
Relativism
Astrology

Divination
Incantations
psychic
dead
Witchcraft's
Occult
Techniques
100
Pan
Sex
Gratification
Satan
Antichrist
worldwide

Chapter 6   *The Rise of Apostasy*

The
Jewish
People
Modern
Technology
Worldwide
Upheaval
Rise
of
Falsehood
Rise
of
Wickedness
themselves
God
Humanism
love
esteem

witchcraft
Wicca
Rise
Apostasy
deliberately
truth
pretend
appearance
turning
away
truth
teachings
sinned
doesn't
same
hell
real
symbol

Money
Materialism
Word
Faith
Movement
monetary
faith
riches
money
free
trinket
rich
nail
cloth
candle
paper
anointing
cornmeal

GENEROUS
force
personal
gain
In
their
greed
get
hold
of
your
money
My
Own
Doctrine
Liberal
Christianity
doctrinal
open
feeling
doctrine
your
own
only
denying
Acceptance
positive
okay

manipulating
sinful
'Father'
'Son'
parent's
child
Mother
Child
Mother
Mother
Child
Human
Judith
correct
gender
accessible
illuminating
empowering
women
Son
Daughter
Lord's
Lady's
her
Judith
She
her
Judith

Judith
she
she
gorilla
Dolphin
Snow
Leopard
Gorilla
beasts
redefined
alcoholism
alternative
adult
entertainment
new
morality
stepping
out
fooling
around
abnormal
development
whatever
rejecting
claim
knowingly
lying

Chapter 7   *One World Religion*

6
5
10
8
7
9

One
World
Religion
Worldwide
Antichrist
Satanically

Watering
Truth
Ecumenical
Absolute
Not
Truth

Watered
Down
Anyone
everyone
claims
cults
compromising
redefining
'divisive'
'unloving'
His
true
Where
eternity
heaven
hell
Worldwide

Assault
Persecution
million
compromise
judgmental
arrogant
narrow-minded
ignorant
old-fashioned
Psycho
dangerous
Obstructionist
hate
Unchristian
hate
bigots
extremists

Welcoming
of
All
Faiths
Interfaithism
All
valid
tolerate
elephant
religious
world
never
out
of
unified

Chapter 8   *One World Government*

Jewish
Technology
Worldwide
Falsehood
Wickedness
Apostasy
Religion
watering
down
Christians
welcoming
all
Government
antichrist
Universal
Congress
Order

absolute
control
fear
manipulation
health-care
child
economy
constitutional
terrorist
environmental
Charter
Constitution
Federation
Government
Supreme
Police
Criminal

Army
NATO
Surveillance
Monitoring
Echelon
England
Canada
Australia
phone
data
radio
"terrorize"
"assassination"
"bomb"
Government

Chapter 9 *One World Economy*

Jewish
People
Modern
Technology
Worldwide
Upheaval
Rise
of
Falsehood
Rise
of
Wickedness
Rise
of
Apostasy
One
World
Religion
One
World
Government

order
surveillance
Economy
Banking
Global
Bank
economic
control
Lending
Monetary
Exchanger
Trade
Ten
Rome
European
Euro
African
Golden
Mandela
North
American

Amero
Currency
Cashless
paper
electronic
check
credit
debit
smart
universal
microchip
readers
standard
all
billion
mandatory
MasterCard
MONDEX
watch
ring
money

Chapter 10 *The Mark of the Beast*

8
2
6
4
9
3
5

7
10
Mark
Beast
worldwide
unsaved
right

forehead
justification
pampered
cool
productive
constructive
willingness

whole
right

right
protected

common
sense

Notes

Chapter 1 *The Jewish People*

1. *Signs That You're Having a Bad Day*
   (Email story) – Source Unknown
2. *The Sign of Israel Returning to the Land*
   (http://www.100prophecies.org/page2.htm)
3. *The Sign of Israel Being Brought Forth in One Day*
   (http://www.bibledesk.com)
4. *The Sign of Israel Being a United Nation Again*
   (http://www.100prophecies.org/page3.htm)
5. *The Sign of Israel's Currency Being the Shekel*
   (http://www.bibledesk.com)
6. *The Sign of Israel Blossoming as a Rose in the Desert*
   (http://www.mastnet.net/~shucka/Israel.htm)
   (http://www.100prophecies.org/page2.htm)
   (http://rr-bb.com/showthread.php?t=27867&highlight=100+reasons)
7. *The Sign of Israel Having a Powerful Military*
   (http://www.mastnet.net/~shucka/Israel.htm)
   (http://www.100prophecies.org/page3.htm)
8. *The Sign of Israel's Temple Having a New Location*
   (http://www.templemount.org/theories.html)
9. *The Sign of Israel Rebuilding Articles for the Temple*
   (http://www.templeinstitute.org)
10. *The Sign of the Return of the Red Heifer*
    (http://www.templeinstitute.org/current-events/RedHeifer/index.html)
11. *The Sign of the Rebirth of the Sanhedrin*
    (http://www.israelnn.com/news.php3?id=70349)
    (http://www.traditioninaction.org/bev/060bev12-20-2004.htm)
    (http://www.israelnationalnews.com/news.php3?id=76624)
12. *Quote from Newspapers About Jewish Expectation of the Messiah*
    (http://www.thejewishpress.com/news_article.asp?article=5370)
    (http://worldnetdaily.com/news/article.asp?ARTICLE_ID=45743)
    (http://www.israelnationalnews.com/News/News.aspx/89850)

Chapter 2   *Modern Technology*

(Email story) – Source Unknown
17. *Story of Senior Citizens*
    (Email story) – Source unknown

Chapter 3   *Worldwide Upheaval*

1. *Story of Steps for a Successful BBQ*
   (Email story) – Source Unknown
2. *Statistics on the Increase of Earthquakes*
   (http://www.countdown.org/armageddon/earthquakes.htm)
   (http://www.mastnet.net/~shucka/6_signs.htm)
   (http://earthquake.usgs.gov/eqcenter/recenteqsus/)
3. *Statistics on the Death Toll of Earthquakes*
   (http://www.lunarpages.com/stargazers/endworld/signs/earthquakes.htm)
4. *Quote Scientists on the Increase of Earthquakes*
   (http://www.countdown.org/armageddon/earthquakes.htm)
5. *Quote Future Fatalities from Earthquakes*
   (http://www.lunarpages.com/stargazers/endworld/signs/earthquakes.htm)
6. *Statistics on Famines*
   (http://www.countdown.org/armageddon/famine.htm)
7. *Statistics on Desertification*
   (http://www.lunarpages.com/stargazers/endworld/signs/famines.htm)
8. *Statistics on China's Desertification*
   (http://thefamily.org/endtime/article.php3?id=4)
9. *Statistics on World Desertification*
   (http://www.cnn.com/TECH/science/9806/21/growing.desert/)
10. *Statistics on Pestilence*
    (http://www.lunarpages.com/stargazers/endworld/signs/pestilenc.htm)
11. *Statistics on AIDS in Africa*
    (http://bible-prophecy.com/plagues.htm)
12. *Statistics on AIDS Contact*
    (http://www.lunarpages.com/stargazers/endworld/signs/pestilenc.htm)
13. *Statistics on the Return of Infectious Diseases*
    (http://www.countdown.org/armageddon/plagues.htm)
14. *Quote on the Overuse of Antibiotics*
    (http://www.lunarpages.com/stargazers/endworld/signs/pestilenc.htm)
15. *Quote from the American Association of Advancement of Science*
    (http://www.lunarpages.com/stargazers/endworld/signs/pestilenc.htm)

16. *Statistics on Wars*
    (http://www.flashnet/~venzor/chapter2signs.htm)
17. *Statistics on Wars After WWII*
    (http://www.lunarpages.com/stargazers/endworld/signs/wars.htm)
18. *Statistics on Wars in 1993*
    (http://www.countdown.org/armageddon/war.htm)
19. *Statistics on Wars in 1995*
    (http://www.lunarpages.com/stargazers/endworld/signs/wars.htm)
20. *Statistics on China's Army*
    (http://www.flashnet/~venzor/chapter2signs.htm)
21. *Statistics on Nuclear Bombs*
    (http://www.bibledesk.com)
22. *Story of Bill Clinton*
    (Email story) – Source Unknown

Chapter Four   *The Rise of Falsehood*

1. *Story of The Top 10 Things Men Know About Women*
   (Email story) – Source Unknown
2. *Quote Sun Myung Moon*
   (http://www.gospelcom.net/apologeticsindex/u05.html)
3. *Quote the Jesus of Siberia*
   (http://www.guardian.co.uk/g2/story/0,3604,721088,00.html)
4. *Quote What's Your Name?*
   (http://news.bbc.co.uk/hi/english/world/americas/newsid_645000/645182.stm)
5. *Quote the Supposed Signs from Lord Maitreya*
   (http://www.shareintl.org/)
6. *Statistics on People in U.S. Claiming to be Jesus Christ*
   (http://members.christhost.com/ResourceCentre/Jesus_lastday_prophecies.ht
   m)
7. *Beliefs of Jose Luis de Jesus Miranda*
   (http://www.allaboutcults.org/jose-luis-de-jesus-miranda.htm)
   (http://www.cnn.com/2007/US/02/16/miami.preacher/)
8. *Statistics on Jerusalem Syndrome*
   (http://news.bbc.co.uk/hi/english/world/middle_east/newsid_577000/577180.
   stm)
9. *Quote Beliefs of New Age Movement*
   (http://www.religioustolerance.org/newage.htm)

(http://www.jeremiahproject.com/prophecy/newage01.html)
(http://www.victorious.org/newage.htm)
10. *Statistics on the Rise of the New Age Movement*
(http://www.religioustolerance.org/newage.htm)
11. *Quote Sierra Club*
(http://www.jeremiahproject.com/prophecy/earth1.html)
12. *Quote Explaining Away the Tribulation*
(http://www.insight-books.com/new/0671759000.html)
(http://www.crystalinks.com/hopi2.html)
13. *Beliefs of the Vegetarian Movement*
(http://www.serv-online.org/)
14. *Quote Interfaith Beliefs of the Vegetarian Movement*
(http://www.serv-online.org/)
(http://www.recipenet.org/health/aboutme.htm)
15. *Quote Beliefs of Supposed Aliens*
(http://www.khouse.org/pages/special_events/alien_encounters/)
16. *The demonic Identity of Supposed Aliens*
(http://www.khouse.org/pages/special_events/alien_encounters/)
17. *Quote Explaining Away the Rapture*
Barbara Marciniak, *Bringers of the Dawn,*
(Santa Fe: Bear & Company Publishing, 1992, Pgs. 166, 167)
18. *Story of Innkeeper's Wife*
(Email story) – Source Unknown

Chapter Five   *The Rise of Wickedness*

1. *Story of Dying Preacher*
(Email story) – Source Unknown
2. *Statistics on Previous Top Ten Discipline Problems in Schools*
(http://www.ohea.org/pubs/pdf/discipline.pdf)
3. *Statistics on the Rise of Wickedness in the U.S.*
Dr. Kent Hovind, *The Age of the Earth,* Video
(Pensacola: Creation Science Evangelism, 1996)
(http://www.geocities.com/Heartland/Village/8759/youth-stats.html)
(http://www.biblesabbath.org/bacchiocchi/endtimewickedness.html)
(http://www.seebo.net/crisis.html)
(http://apnews.myway.com/article/20080228/D8V3KF5O0.html)
4. *Quote Beliefs of Humanist Manifest I & II*

(http://www.SecularHumanism.org)

5. *Quote Humanist Agenda*
(http://www.lunarpages.com/stargazers/endworld/signs/occult.htm)

6. *Behavior of Sigmund Freud*
B.R. Hergenhahn, *An Introduction To Theories Of Personalities*,
(Upper Saddle River: Prentice Hall, 1999, Pg. 23)

7. *Behavior of Carl Jung*
B.R. Hergenhahn, *An Introduction To Theories Of Personalities*,
(Upper Saddle River: Prentice Hall, 1999, Pgs. 65, 66-67)

8. *Beliefs of Abraham Maslow & Carl Rogers*
B.R. Hergenhahn, *An Introduction To Theories Of Personalities*,
(Upper Saddle River: Prentice Hall, 1999, Pgs. 467-529)

9. *Banned Behavior from Self-Esteem Teaching*
Tucker Carlson, *Go Ahead, Hurt My Feelings*,
(Reader's Digest: August 2002, Pgs. 43, 44, 46)

10. *Self-delusion from Self-Esteem Teaching*
Tucker Carlson, *Go Ahead, Hurt My Feelings*,
(Reader's Digest: August 2002, Pg. 46)

11. *Beliefs of Witchcraft*
(http://www.gospelcom.net/apologeticsindex/w02.html)
(http://www.gospelcom.net/apologeticsindex/w04.html)

12. *Psychologists Using Witchcraft*
(http://www.gospelcom.net/apologeticsindex/news/an200215b.html)

13. *Witch Covens Allowed in U.S. Army*
(http://www.bible-prophecy.com/apostasy3.htm#Current)

14. *The Identity of Pan*
(http://www.forerunner.com/champion/X0044_Witchcraft_and_satan.html)

15. *Statistics on Wicca*
(http://www.gospelcom.net/cgi-apologeticsindex/dbman/db.cgi?db=
default&uid=default&keyword=wicca&mh=10&sb=4&so=descend&view_r
ecords=View+Records&nh=3)

16. *Story of Going Door to Door*
(Email story) – Source Unknown

Chapter Six   *The Rise of Apostasy*

1. *Story of Man Eating a Bowl of Chili*
(Email story) – Source Unknown

2. *Statistics on the Rise of Apostasy*
   (http://www.barna.org/)
3. *Church Growth Teachings Versus the Bible*
   (http://www.fundamentalbiblechurch.org/Foundation/fbcsdlbk.htm)
4. *Quotes from Word of Faith Teachers*
   Hank Hanegraaff, *Christianity In Crisis*
   (Eugene: Harvest House Publishers, 1993, Pgs. 11, 21, 24-25, 26-27)
5. *Different So-Called Miracle Trinkets*
   (http://www.bible.ca/tongues-photogallery-pentacostal-trinkets.htm)
6. *Quote on The New Jesus*
   Tony Campolo, *Carpe Diem*,
   (Dallas: Word Publishing, 1994, Pgs. 46, 47)
7. *Statistics on Signs & Wonders Experiences Versus the Occult*
   (http://www.bible.ca/tongues-kundalini-shakers-charismatics.htm)
8. *Quotes from New Versions of the Bible*
   Ravi Zacharias, *Deliver Us From Evil*
   (Dallas: Word Publishing, 1996, Pgs. 52-53)
   (http://www.worldnetdaily.com/news/printer-friendly.asp?ARTICLE_ID
   =44563)
   (http://www.worldnetdaily.com/news/article.asp?ARTICLE_ID=54518)
9. *Quote on Redefining Sinful Behavior*
   Jeffrey A. Baker, *Cheque Mate the Game of Princes*
   (St. Petersburg: The Baker Group Inc., 1993, Pgs. 206-207)
10. *Story of Hockey Rivalry*
    (Email story) – Source Unknown

Chapter Seven   *One World Religion*

1. *List of Weird Things in Life*
   (Email story) – Source Unknown
2. *Definition of Ecumenicalism*
   (http://www.jeremiahproject.com/prophecy/ecumen01.html)
3. *Quote Salad Bar Religion*
   (http://www.gospelcom.net/apologeticsindex/c43.html)
4. *Statistics on Hitler Killing Christians*
   (http://www.666beast.com/countdown.htm)
5. *Statistics on Christian Persecution*
   (http://www.jeremiahproject.com/prophecy/warxian.html)

6. *Statistics on Yearly Christian Deaths*
   (http://www.lunarpages.com/stargazers/endworld/signs/persecution.htm)
7. *Statistics on Total Christian Deaths*
   (http://www.jeremiahproject.com/prophecy/warxian.html)
8. *Evidence of the Rise of Christian Persecution in the U.S.*
   (http://countdown.org/end/apostasy_03.htm)
   (http://countdown.org/end/apostasy_05.htm)
   (http://www.jeremiahproject.com/prophecy/warxian.html)
9. *Quote on Reading the Bible in Jail Rather than in School*
   (http://www.lunarpages.com/stargazers/endworld/signs/fallaway.htm)
10. *Claims that Christians are Judgmental*
    (http://www.jeremiahproject.com/prophecy/warxian.html)
11. *Claims that Christians are Dangerous*
    (http://countdown.org/end/apostasy_03.htm)
    (http://www.jeremiahproject.com/prophecy/warxian.html)
    (http://www.cuttingedge.org/NEWS/n1861.cfm)
12. *Quote from Janet Reno*
    (http://kenraggio.com/KRPN-UnitedReligions.htm)
13. *Timeline of the Rise of a One World Religion*
    (http://www.endtimeinfo.net/religion/religiousleader.html)
    (http://bible-prophecy.com/religions.htm)
    (http://www.fastboot.com/one_world_religion.html)
    (http://www.lamblion.com/prophecy/signs/Signs-06.html)
    (http://www.millenniumpeacesummit.org/summit_outcomes.html)
    (http://www.orthodoxinfo.com/ecumenism/video2.htm)
    (http://www.understandthetimes.org/topics/oneworldreligion_archive
    .shtml)
    (http://www.understandthetimes.org/topics/oneworldreligion.shtml)
    (http://www.worldpeacesummit.net/)
    (http://www.swarthmore.edu/Library/peace/DG051-099/DG078WCRP
    .html)
    (http://www.religionsforpeace.org/)
14. *Quote from Ted Turner*
    (http://www.endtimeinfo.net/religion/religiouspeace.html)
15. *New Program from Prince Charles*
    (http://bible-prophecy.com/religions.htm)
16. *Quote from Al Gore*
    (http://www.jeremiahproject.com/prophecy/ecumen01.html)
17. *Occult's Expectation for a One World Religion*

(http://www.cuttingedge.org/n1052.html)
18. *Story of Driver's Day Going from Bad to Worse*
(Email story) – Source Unknown

Chapter Eight   *One World Government*

1. *Story of Old Cowboy's Advice*
(Email story) – Source Unknown
2. *Quote of Everything is a Crisis*
(http://www.jeremiahproject.com/prophecy/nworder.html)
3. *Information on the Earth Charter*
(http://www.earthcharter.org)
4. *Information on the Constitution for the Federation Earth*
(http://www.wcpagren.org/cnfdeart.dir/contents.html)
5. *Information on the World Criminal Court*
(http://www.portal.telegraph.co.uk/news/main.jhtml?xml=/news/2002/06/26/
wicc26.xml&sSheet=/news/2002/06/26/ixworld.html&secureRefresh=true&
_requestid=97738)
(http://www.newsmax.com/archives/articles/2002/5/6/154932.shtml)
6. *Quote Tony Blair*
(http://www.freedaily.com/articles/990424n1.html)
7. *Quotes on the New World Order*
(http://www.lunarpages.com/stargazers/endworld/fin-signs/news/global
news.htm)
(http://bible-prophecy.com/nwo2.htm)
(http://babylonmysteryreligion.com/unitednationsagenda.htm)
8. *Information on the Word Heritage Protection Program*
(http://whc.unesco.org/nwhc/pages/home/pages/homepage.htm)
(http://www.crossroad.to/text/articles/whpwans97.html)
9. *Information on the World Food Summit*
(http://www.fao.org/wfs/index_en.htm)
(http://www.radioliberty.com/kjos3.htm)
10. *Information on Agenda 21*
(http://www.un.org/esa/sustdev/agenda21text.htm)
(http://wwwcrossroad.to/text/articles/la21_198.html)
11. *Information on the Biodiversity Treaty*
(http://www.epi.freedom.org/mapmabwh.htm)
(http://www.epi.freedom.org/mapwild.htm)

12. *Information on Global Diversity Assessment*
(http://www.wri.org/biodiv/gba-unpr.html)
(http://www.radioliberty.com/kjos3.htm)
13. *Statistics on World Abortions*
(http://www.radioliberty.com/pca.htm)
14. *Quotes on Reducing the World's Population*
(http://www.radioliberty.com/pca.htm)
15. *Time Goal for Reducing the World's Population*
(http://www.croassroad.to/text/articles/whpwans97.html)
16. *Information on Executive Orders*
(http://www.crossroad.to/text/articles/nis1196.html)
17. *New Surveillance Technology*
(http://countdown.org/end/big_brother_13.htm)
(http://countdown.org/end/big_brother_12.htm)
(http://countdown.org/end/big_brother_13.htm)
(http://countdown.org/end/big_brother_09.htm)
(http://www.khouse.org/articles/political/20010801-360.html)
(http://countdown.org/end/big_brother_02.htm)
(http://www.mvcf.com/news/cache/00065/)
(http://countdown.org/end/big_brother_06.htm)
18. *Quote on Usage of Surveillance Cameras*
(http://www.usatoday.com/life/cyber/tech/cti856.htm)
19. *Statistics on England's Surveillance Canopy*
(http://www.usatoday.com/life/cyber/tech/cti856.htm)
(http://www.thetruthseeker.co.uk/article.asp?ID=1421)
20. *Quote on England's Surveillance Canopy*
(http://countdown.org/end/big_brother_05.htm)
21. *Information on Japan's Surveillance Technology*
(http://countdown.org/end/big_brother_12.htm)
22. *Information on Project Echelon*
(http://countdown.org/end/big_brother_08.htm)
(http://www.khouse.org/articles/currentevents/20000401-213.html)
(http://www.mvcf.com/news/cache/00065/)
23. *Quote Mike Frost*
(http://www.mvcf.com/news/cache/00065/)
24. *Timeline of a One World Government*
(http://www.khouse.org/articles/political/19970301-90.html)
(http://bible-prophecy.com/now.htm)

(http://en.wikipedia.org/wiki/New_World_Order_(conspiracy)#New_World_Order_timeline)
(http://www.threeworldwars.com/nwo-timeline2.htm)
(http://www.understandthetimes.org/topics/oneworldgov_archive.shtml)
(http://www.understandthetimes.org/topics/oneworldgov.shtml)
25. *Quote Georgia Guidestones*
(http://www.radioliberty.com/stones.htm)
26. *Story of Clown in Pain*
(Email story) – Source Unknown

Chapter Nine   *One World Economy*

1. *Story of Biased News Headlines*
(Email story) – Source Unknown
2. *Information on the World Bank*
(http://www.worldbank.org)
3. *Information on the International Monetary Fund*
(http://www.imf.org)
4. *Information on SWIFT*
(http://www.swift.com)
5. *Information on the World Trade Organization*
(http://www.wto.org)
(http://www.mvcf.com/news/cache/00438/)
6. *Information on the Birth of the Euro*
(http://www.euro.gov.uk/home.asp?f=1)
7. *Information on Tony Blair's Support of the Euro*
(http://www.mvcf.com/news/cache/00035/)
8. *Quote from Robert Mundell*
(http://www.mvcf.com/news/cache/00185/)
9. *Timeline of a One World Economy*
(http://bible-prophecy.com/smart2.htm)
(http://www.khouse.org/articles/political/19970301-90.html)
(http://www.globalcommunity.org)
(http://www.globalexchange.org)
(http://www.mvcf.com/news/cache/00356/)
(http://www.understandthetimes.org/topics/oneworldgov_archive.shtml)
(http://www.understandthetimes.org/topics/oneworldgov.shtml)

(http://www.understandthetimes.org/topics/techmoney.shtml)
10. *Quote from Global Governance*
    (http://www.mvcf.com/news/cache/00447/)
11. *Information on the Ten Economic Kingdoms*
    (http://themustardseed.home.mindspring.com/n16-11.htm)
12. *Information on Foreign Troops on American Soil*
    (http://www.blackwebportal.com/forums/viewmessages.cfm?Forum
    =37&Topic=1113)
13. *Information on the African Union*
    (http://www.worldnetdaily.com/news/article.asp?ARTICLE_ID=57018)
14. *Information on the North American Union*
    (http://www.worldnetdaily.com/news/article.asp?ARTICLE_ID=57980)
    (http://www.wnd.com/news/article.asp?ARTICLE_ID=50618)
15. *Information on Various Unions*
    (http://en.wikipedia.org/wiki/Pacific_Union)
    (http://en.wikipedia.org/wiki/Union_of_South_American_Nations)
    (http://en.wikipedia.org/wiki/Asian_Union)
    (http://en.wikipedia.org/wiki/Mediterranean_Union)
16. *Various Uses for Smart Cards*
    (http://bible-prophecy.com/smart2.htm)
17. *Quote on Decreased Crime from the Usage of Smart Cards*
    (http://www.sfasu.edu/finance/FINCASH.HTM)
18. *Information on the Personal Electronic Transfer*
    (http://www.geocities.com/Heartland/Pointe/4171/profeticword.html)
19. *Information on Smart Card Readers*
    (http://bible-prophecy.com/smart2.htm)
20. *Information on Smart Card Readers in Computers*
    (http://www.networkusa.org/fingerprint/page5a/fp-pki-spock.html)
21. *Information on Cell Phones to Pay for Purchases*
    (http://bible-prophecy.com/smart2.htm)
22. *Quote on Radio Frequency Burgers*
    (http://www.endtimeinfo.net/cashless/cellphone.html)
23. *Statistics on the Amount of Smart Cards Issued*
    (http://bible-prophecy.com/smart2.htm)
24. *Information on England Issuing Smart Cards*
    (http://bible-prophecy.com/smart2.htm)
    (http://www.egov.vic.gov.au/index.php?env=-categories:m1397-1-1-8-s-
    0&reset=1)
25. *Information on Britney Spears Issuing Smart Cards*

(http://bible-prophecy.com/smart2.htm)
26. *Information on the Pentagon Issuing Smart Cards*
(http://bible-prophecy.com/smart2.htm)
27. *Information on MasterCard's Plan for Smart Cards*
(http://bible-prophecy.com/smart2.htm)
28. *Information on MasterCard's Purchase of MONDEX*
(http://www.geocities.com/Heartland/Pointe/4171/profeticword.html)
29. *Information on MONDEX*
(http://bible-prophecy.com/smart2.htm)
30. *Quote on MONDEX Becoming a Global Standard*
(http://www.geocities.com/Heartland/Pointe/4171/profeticword.html)
(http://www.mondexusa.com)
31. *Information on VISA Putting Smart Card Microchips in Watches & Rings*
(http://bible-prophecy.com/smart2.htm)
32. *Story of Man Telling a Blonde Joke*
(Email story) – Source Unknown

Chapter Ten   *The Mark of the Beast*

1. *Story of Nasty Bug*
(Email story) – Source Unknown
2. *Information on Motorola Satellites*
(http://www.endtimeinfo.net/mark/rfid.html)
3. *Information on Satellites Monitoring Boat Traffic*
(http://countdown.org/end/big_brother_05.html)
4. *Information on Satellites Monitoring Garbage Men*
(http://countdown.org/end/big_brother_04.html)
5. *Information on the Internet in the Sky*
(http://www.bible-prophecy.com/techmark.htm)
6. *Information on Acxiom Database*
(http://www.bible-prophecy.com/mark.htm)
7. *Information on the Amount of Information in Axciom's Database*
(http://countdown.org/end/big_brother_01.html)
8. *Information on the Amount of Databases*
(http://countdown.org/end/big_brother_06.html)
9. *Different Kinds of Personal Identification Devices*
(http://countdown.org/end/big_brother_04.html)
(http://countdown.org/end/big_brother_02.html)

(http://countdown.org/end/big_brother_13.html)
(http://www.mvcf.com/news/cache/00440/)
(http://www.countdown.org/end/mark_of_the_beast_05.html)
(http://www.mvcf.com/news/cache/00400/)
(http://countdown.org/end/big_brother_11.html)
(http://www.mvcf.com/news/cache/00431/)
(http://www.endtimeinfo.net/mark/eyeball.html)
(http://www.privacy.org/pi/reprots/biometric.html)
(http://www.endtimeinfo.net/cashless/fingerprint.html)
10. *Information on Tracking Students*
    (http://countdown.org/end/big_brother_13.html)
11. *Information on Digital Angel*
    (http://wwwadsx.com)
12. *Information on FDA Approval of Digital Angel*
    (http://www.bible-prophecy.com/mark2.htm)
13. *Examples of Being More Pampered with Implants*
    (http://www.thefamily.org/endtime/article.php3?id=12)
    (http://countdown.org/end/big_brother_06.html)
    (http://www.bible-prophecy.com/smart2.htm)
    (http://countdown.org/end/big_brother_04.html)
    (http://countdown.org/end/big_brother_02.html)
    (http://www.lunarpages.com/stargazers/endworld/fin-signs/news/ chip.htm)
14. *Articles on Being Pampered with Implants*
    (http://countdown.org/end/big_brother_06.html)
    (http://countdown.org/end/big_brother_04.html)
15. *Examples of Being More Productive with Implants*
    (http://www.bible-prophecy.com/mark.htm)
    (http://countdown.org/end/big_brother_05.html)
    (http://countdown.org/end/big_brother_03.html)
    (http://www.digitalangel.net/medical.asp)
    (http://www.lunarpages.com/stargazers/endworld/fin-signs/news/
    chip.htm)
    (http://countdown.org/end/big_brother_01.html)
    (http://countdown.org/end/big_brother_07.html)
16. *Examples of Being More Protected with Implants*
    (http://www.digitalangel.net/consumer.asp)
    (http://countdown.org/end/big_brother_03.html)
    (http://www.geocities.com/Heartland/Ridge/1428/mark.html)
17. *Various People Who are Positive about Implants*

(http://www.bible-prophecy.com/mark2.htm)
(http://countdown.org/end/big_brother_07.html)
(http://wwwadsx.com/news/2002/042602.html)
(http://wwwadsx.com/news/2002/081602.html)

18. *Information on Mandatory Chipping of Pets*
(http://countdown.org/end/big_brother_03.html)
19. *Quote from Kevin Warwick*
(http://countdown.org/end/big_brother_06.html)
20. *Information on the Jacob's Family Being Chipped*
(http://www.abcnews.go.com/sections/scitech/TechTV/techtv_chipfamily020510.html)
21. *Information on People's Willingness to be Chipped*
(http://www.millenniumhope.info/article1023.html)
22. *Article on the Benefits of Being Chipped*
(http://countdown.org/end/big_brother_07.html)
23. *Article on the History of Chipping Propaganda*
(http://www.newswithviews.com/guest_opinion/guest54.htm)
24. *Polling Data on the Willingness of People Being Chipped*
(http://www.msnbc.msn.com/id/15221100/)
25. *Quote from Scott Silverman*
(http://www.miami.com/mld/miami/business/3240630.htm)
26. *Quote from Senator Joseph Biden on Implants*
(http://portland.indymedia.org/en/2005/09/325974.shtml)
27. *Information on the Immigration Control Act*
(http://www.endtimeinfo.net/mark/rfid.html)
28. *List of Special Executive Orders*
(http://www.geocities.com/SouthBeach/Lagoon/1780/exec.html)
(http://www.fema.gov)
29. *European Union's Plans for a Universal Identification*
(http://www.endtimeinfo.net/mark/euid.html)
30. *Japan's Plans for a Universal Identification*
(http://asia.news.yahoo.com/020805/reuters/asia-118809.html)
31. *United Nation's Plans for a Universal Identification*
(http://www.smh.com.au/breaking/2001/12/14/FFX058CU6VC.html)
32. *Quote from Dr. Carl Sanders*
(http://www.lunarpages.com/stargazers/endworld/fin-signs/news/chip.htm)
(http://meltingpot.fortunecity.com/chicon/321/mark_of_the_beast.htm)
33. *Story of Blonde Woman and Shepherd*

(Email story) – Source Unknown
34. *Quote from Martin Niemoeller*
(http://www.radioliberty.com/pca.htm)

CPSIA information can be obtained at www.ICGtesting.com
Printed in the USA
LVOW05s0404130214

373384LV00002B/571/P